SPY THE
STORY OF MODERN
ESPIONAGE

SPY THE STORY OF MODERN ESPIONAGE

Clifford Irving

and

Herbert Burkholz

MACMILLAN PUBLISHING CO., INC.
NEW YORK

For Howard and Matthew,
Joshua and Ned

Macmillan Publishing Co., Inc.
866 Third Avenue, New York, N.Y. 10022
Collier-Macmillan Canada, Ltd., Toronto, Ontario

Library of Congress catalog card number: 77-78080

Printed in the United States of America

10   9   8   7   6   5   4   3   2

CONTENTS

In the affairs of state, as in the
affairs of men, the sweetest smile is
on the face of the deceiver.

—Jean le Malchanceux

1 THE PRIVATE WORLD OF ESPIONAGE

There was a heavy mist rising that February morning in 1962, a mist that swirled as high as the railings of Berlin's Glienicker Bridge. It covered the roadway and most of the bridge itself in layers of soiled cotton wool, and almost obscured the two groups of uniformed men who approached each other from opposite ends of the span. The two parties advanced slowly with measured, invisible steps, for the waist-high mist concealed their legs and they seemed to float through space without effort. But the foggy morning and the wet roadway were only minor reasons for their caution. East met West at the center of the bridge—East Berlin and West Berlin—and the men who met that morning were involved in a mission of great political delicacy. And so they advanced slowly, each group reluctant to be the first to reach the line that marked the border.

As if their pace had been regulated by some master puppeteer, the two groups arrived at the center of the bridge together. A few gruff questions were asked; responses were made in the same tone of voice. Then one man from each group stepped over the line and joined the opposing party. At a given signal, Colonel Rudolf Abel of the KGB, the Russian intelligence organization, a slight, bespectacled man who looked no more dangerous than a neighborhood grocer, left his American captors to join the group of Russians waiting for him. At the same time Francis Gary Powers, whose young, healthy, stocky appearance was in startling contrast to that of Abel, crossed the line to join the Americans. A few more words completed the transaction, and the master puppeteer again pulled the strings. As if at a spoken command, the two groups wheeled and marched away through the fog, away from each other, from the bridge, and from the first exchange of acknowledged spies in modern history.

The two men who were exchanged, Rudolf Abel and Francis Powers, were both spies. They both were experts in their respective fields, but there the similarity between the two men ended. The differences between them were far more interesting than their common profession, for between them they represented a major revolution in espionage technique. The harmless-looking Colonel Abel was a master spy in the classic tradition. Meticulously trained and prepared for his job, he had been the resident director of Russian espionage in the United States until his capture by the FBI in 1957. He had served less than five years of a thirty-year sentence when he was exchanged for Francis Powers.

By contrast, the young American represented a new generation of espionage, one which depended more on science and technology than on invisible ink, meetings on shadowed street corners, and secret codes. Powers was nothing more than an airborne chauffeur, trained to fly a highly sophisticated aircraft at an altitude of ninety thousand feet over the Soviet Union; trained to press the right button at the right time so that cameras would roll and other sensitive equipment would record vital information for the Central Intelligence Agency. He performed this function expertly for four years, and then on the morning of May Day 1960 the bright orange flash of an exploding missile lit up the sky over the Soviet city of Sverdlovsk. That rocket brought his U-2 spy plane fluttering to earth, brought Francis Gary Powers to a Russian prison, and ushered in a new era in the history of espionage. For the first time, a major power—the United States of America—openly acknowledged its spying.

Traditionally, spies are disowned by their countries. The agents in the field know this, and when captured they expect nothing from their masters at home. Indeed, the Soviet Union reacted in this traditional fashion when Colonel Abel was captured: they not only disowned him, they refused to admit that such a person existed. President Eisenhower shattered this precedent, however, by publicly assuming responsibility for

Powers after the U-2 flight. At the time he did so he was severely criticized in diplomatic circles for openly admitting to a clandestine operation. Years later he gave his reasons in his memoirs, *The White House Years*:

> Francis Gary Powers was no individual traveler sneaking across borders between guards and living in concealed garrets in the land of a potential enemy; Powers had been apprehended thirteen hundred miles within Soviet territory, flying a piece of expensive machinery, equipped with the most intricate set of cameras. . . . In the diplomatic field it was routine practice to deny responsibility for an embarrassing occurrence when there is even a one percent chance of being believed but when the world can entertain not the slightest doubt of the facts there is no point in trying to evade the issue.

Because of this admission, the U-2 incident made the world suddenly aware of something it had dimly known, but had preferred to ignore: that the two major espionage establishments, the Russian and the American, could openly collide, and with spectacular results. International espionage, which had always operated like an iceberg, seven eighths concealed from view, now became subject to worldwide scrutiny, and the names of secret organizations became as familiar to the public as household words. It amounted to nothing less than an espionage revolution, for the U-2 affair educated millions to the grim everyday realities of spying.

The organization which Rudolf Abel served so faithfully, the Komitet Gosudarstvennoi Bezopasnosti, better known as the KGB, is one of the two major instruments of secret power in the Russian state. Allen W. Dulles, who as head of the CIA competed with the KGB for eight years, described the organization in *The Craft of Intelligence* as "a multipurpose, clandestine arm of power . . . more than a secret police organization, more than an intelligence and counter-intelligence organization. It is an instrument for subversion, manipulation and violence, for secret intervention in the affairs of other countries."

What Dulles did not say, however, is that this quite accurate description applies equally to the counterparts of the KGB in other countries: his own Central Intelligence Agency, the British MI5 and MI6, the Social Affairs Department of Communist China, and the KGB's own rival within Soviet Russia, the Chief Intelligence Directorate of the Red Army General Staff, known as the GRU. All of these agencies are engaged daily in a silent struggle which takes place largely out of sight, but which affects the factory worker in Detroit as much as the businessman in London, the student in Heidelberg, the diplomat in New York, and the soldier in the Vietnam jungle. No one living in the modern world can escape the impact of espionage, and if the world of secret intelligence is a world unto itself, it is one which is woven so firmly into the fabric of our society that it stains the cloth a distinctive hue. Red, white, and blue, or just plain red, modern espionage colors the meanest details of our lives and, for better or worse, will continue to do so—for the espionage establishment is an integral part of our time.

No matter what its original purpose, the modern intelligence organization has become a source of great secret power within its own society, shaping and prodding history, and provoking events to the point where the establishment comes close to controlling the government which created it; the tail wagging the dog. In Russia, KGB pressure helped to bring about the downfall of Nikita Khrushchev; in England, the Profumo affair spelled the end of Harold Macmillan's career; Charles de Gaulle's grandeur was tarnished by the Ben Barka case; in Canada, the government of Prime Minister Lester Pearson was shaken by the Munsinger matter; and in the United States, John F. Kennedy had his Bay of Pigs.

This power to move and to shake world events is the obverse of the romantic side of the coin we see when we read any one of the current crop of spy thrillers. Most of what is written about espionage today is fantasy, for as Soviet master spy Rudolf Abel put it, "Intelligence work is not just adventure, not some kind of stunt, not gay trips abroad." In fact, modern intelligence work is mostly the cold, analytical gathering and evaluation of information from all sorts of sources, the most mundane often being the most valuable. It is work for fine minds, capable of careful assessment, and the espionage establishments of all the major world powers tend to attract the elite, privileged, and better-educated members of their societies. In the United States and Britain, intelligence officials most often come from wealthy, upper-class families whose young men are more interested in public service than in amassing further wealth. Their Russian counterparts are members of the Soviet elite: dedicated members of the Komsomol youth group and the Communist Party whose spotless records have promoted them into positions of power. Thus, although the American and Soviet organizations differ in size and in function, they are remarkably alike in overall purpose and in the type of qualified person they recruit.

It is in their functions that the two organizations differ most, and it is this point which is often confusing to the uninitiated student of cloak and dagger. One of the problems in assessing the size of the KGB is that it combines under one tent the functions of the CIA, the FBI, the Secret Service, the U. S. Border Patrol, and several other agencies that do not even exist in our governmental structure. In the Western democracies, two separate organizations which function individually and with a clear division of responsibility have been entrusted with the twin complements of state security. One is a counterintelligence agency whose job it is to track down foreign spies operating within the country; the other is an organization for maintaining espionage agents in foreign countries. Thus, in France the first is represented by the Deuxième Bureau, the second by Intelligence; in the U.S.A., by the FBI and the CIA; and in Great Britain by MI5 and MI6, the latter popularly known as the British Secret Service. In the Soviet Union, however, the two functions are combined, despite the apparent contradiction that foreign espionage should be the responsibility of a department charged with *internal* security. It has always been a Russian contention that their foreign espionage has never been an external, offensive activity, but rather one designed to defend the security of the state. This position contains a certain foundation of logic, and a good case can be made for the logical and practical superiority of the Soviet method over the dual system. Counterespionage and espionage have a common basis, for counterespionage simply sets spies to catch spies, and its spy catchers use many of the same operational methods as do the spies they are out to catch.

This duality in the Soviet spy system has its historical roots in the Russian Revolution itself, when the Extraordinary Commission for the Struggle Against Counter-Revolution and Sabotage—called Cheka—was formed by Felix Dzershinsky, whose name now graces the Moscow street in which is located the KGB headquarters and its infamous Lubianka Prison. During the hectic days of the Revolution the Cheka had two tasks of equal importance. The first was to oppose the activities of all counter-revolutionaries, White Army spies, and secret agents of foreign countries; the second was to organize a Secret Service abroad. However, the opposition to the regime was so strong during the first few years of Bolshevik rule that the main effort of the Cheka had to be concentrated on internal security. The result was that the second objective suffered, and the organization of a foreign Secret Service lagged badly during that period. It was only when the struggle with the White Russian forces came to an end early in 1922 that the Cheka was renamed the State

Political Administration (Gosudarstvennoye Politiches-koye Upravlenye, or GPU) and was able to turn its attention to activities abroad. By 1924 it had established its networks and refined its procedures to the point that Soviet foreign espionage, on the scale to which we have now become accustomed, may be said to date from that year. This development was accompanied by yet another change in name, and with the addition of the title Obiedinennoye (United), the organization became the OGPU.

The OGPU operated until 1934 when its functions were taken over by a department of the People's Commissariat for Internal Affairs, the NKVD. This arrangement lasted until just before the outbreak of World War II when the department was raised to the level of a commissariat itself, becoming known as the NKGB. After Hitler's invasion of Russian territory, however, the NKGB was demoted to its previous departmental rank, and remained at that level until 1943, when it was once again elevated to a commissariat, changing its title to MGB in 1946 when all commissariats were renamed as ministries. After the death of Stalin in 1953 and the subsequent fall of the bloodthirsty MGB chief Lavrenti Beria, the Soviet espionage system was again united with the Ministry of Internal Affairs. This lasted for a year, until March 1954, when it became a separate unit again under yet another title, the Committee of State Security, or KGB, which is how it functions today.

This, then, is the vast, complicated, and powerful espionage, intelligence, and police organization which has its headquarters near the Kremlin at 2 Dzershinsky Street in the Lubianka building. The headquarters is actually two buildings with the facade remodeled to conceal where they join. One building is the KGB prison; the other contains the administrative offices. The massive stone structure is innocuous in appearance, resembling nothing more than a large office building, as indeed it might since it housed an insurance company during Czarist times. In fact, more than this one parallel can be made between the KGB and a large commercial company. Since the death of Stalin the KGB has become an increasingly professional organization, less identified with the personality of a particular chief than in the past. In present-day Russia, important fallen political leaders are not executed, they are exiled and isolated. Accordingly, the life expectancy of an intelligence chief has improved considerably, and the ranks of the KGB are protected to some extent from the decimating purges that characterized Soviet intelligence in Stalin's time. One result of this new professional status is that the KGB is able to operate as an accepted part of Soviet life and not merely as an agency of terror. Indeed, the organization is so integrated into communal activities that it maintains its own soccer team, the Dynamo. The Dynamo Sports Club is the KGB club in Moscow and is one of the two largest in the Soviet Union, its chief rival being Spartak, the Red Army Sports Club. Top Dynamo players have nominal jobs with the KGB but are practically professional athletes, much like football scholarship students at large American universities.

The internal organization of the KGB is a matter of some dispute. American intelligence agencies receive periodic information on this subject from defectors, but the data is fragmentary, conflicting, and often out of date. This much, however, is known. The headquarters of the KGB, known colloquially as "The Center," is divided into two directorates, each led by a chief of deputy-ministerial rank. The First Directorate is roughly comparable to the intelligence agencies found in other countries; the Second Directorate is concerned with the internal affairs of Soviet Russia.

The First Directorate is divided into six main divisions. The first of these is the Foreign Division, whose functions make it the most important since it controls all secret agents and assembles the results obtained by the networks. In addition, it directs intelligence research and disseminates the information collected. Under its direct control is the Operational Division, which, as the name implies, directs the actual operation of the agents, controls the networks, and selects the agents to be sent abroad. The Operational Division is also in charge of recruitment of potential agents, and maintains its own people in every Russian embassy, consulate, or other official delegation abroad.

The third division is Communications, a title which covers everything from the latest innovations in high-speed radiotelegraphy to a microdot message so small it could be placed over the period at the end of this sentence. The operational techniques of this division encompass the most advanced results of the technology—

we will deal with them in detail later. In addition, the Communications Division is responsible for agent rescue operations. If an agent is compromised and must make a rapid departure from his territory, this division organizes the escape route. It was this arm of Soviet intelligence which arranged the escapes of such spies operating in England as Burgess and Maclean and, eventually, Kim Philby.

The fourth, or Secret Division, is actually the documentation service of the KGB. It can supply every conceivable kind of forged document that an agent is likely to need, and in addition can produce any uniform, cap, or badge it might be asked for. One of its sections has the function of preparing cover stories for agents, while yet another supplies the necessary codes, inks, and radio apparatus which the Communications Division may require.

The Information Division does exactly what its name suggests. It collects every scrap of information it can lay its hands on concerning the social, cultural, economic, and political affairs of every country in which it operates. Every foreign newspaper, from the *New York Times* to the most obscure scientific periodical published in Washington or Tokyo, is read by this division, and it listens in on radio broadcasts on a worldwide scale. However, the most interesting section of this division is the Index, which is a vast collection of biographies of everyone who might, even remotely, be of use to Soviet espionage. Besides the usual background information, the Index also keeps a record of a man's political views, his financial circumstances, his debts, and his personal habits. This last is most important, and any scandal which can be discovered about a man is faithfully recorded. Is he having trouble paying off the mortgage on his house? Might he be a homosexual? Has his wife committed some kind of indiscretion? Does his college-age son use drugs? The main object is to discover his weaknesses as well as strengths, since scandal and weakness may be used as twin levers on the reluctant collaborator. It has been estimated that at least two hundred and fifty people are employed in keeping the Index up to date, and the accuracy and efficiency of this section have been testified to on many occasions.

The sixth division of the First Directorate is involved with the training of agents, a subject so important that we will deal with it at length in subsequent chapters.

So far we have examined only the First Directorate of the Soviet Secret Service, and it should be understood that the counterparts of its organization and operational procedures may be found in all the secret services of the Western democracies. No country has a patent on efficiency, and modern espionage establishments tend to develop along the same efficient lines. The Second Directorate, however, is something quite different. Its counterpart will not be found outside of Soviet Russia or its satellites, simply because the greater part of its functions would not be tolerated so openly in a democratic society. Few sweet-smelling roses grow in the jungle of modern espionage, but in the Western democracies the functions of the Second Directorate are accomplished sub rosa, without official knowledge, and not as a recognized part of governmental procedure.

The Propaganda Division of the Second Directorate possesses a responsibility which belies its straightforward and relatively innocent name. Besides performing the routine functions of political propaganda, the division maintains contact with the Communist Parties of other countries, and is particularly active in Latin America and other areas where local parties have been suppressed by official action. The division employs its own agents—an important departure from normal procedure—whose main tasks are to gather political intelligence and to create local subversive groups for future revolutionary action.

The second, or Individual Division, is the one which keeps a check on the reliability of Soviet citizens at home and abroad. Similar checks are kept on Soviet officials working abroad, from an ambassador down to the embassy chauffeur, who may, in fact, be a high-ranking member of the First Directorate's Foreign Division. In addition, all delegations that travel outside Russia, all groups of athletes, musicians, or engineers, have agents of the Individual Division attached to them. And finally, in the curious mirror image world of Russian intelligence, the agents of this division also maintain surveillance on all agents working for the other divisions and sections of Soviet espionage. It may sound like an amusing game—spies spying on spies—but it is not; it is a deadly serious and dangerous business.

The third division of the Second Directorate, the

Allied Division, controls the intelligence activities of Russia's East European allies. The security police and espionage services of Poland, Czechoslovakia, Romania, Hungary, and Bulgaria are supervised by representatives from this division, and in the case of East Germany, these departments are actually directed by Russian officials. Although these so-called satellite countries carry out espionage activities on their own accounts, they also operate on behalf of Soviet espionage through this division. In many cases the intelligence gathered by agents of the satellite nations goes direct to Moscow Center, and the government of the country of origin—Poland or Hungary, for example—is never aware of it.

The fourth division of the Second Directorate is the Special Division, one of the oldest departments of Soviet espionage, and one which was set up by Dzershinsky to liquidate the enemies of the Revolution by violence and murder. Between 1932 and 1936 it was Josef Stalin's personal instrument for ridding himself of his opponents; during World War II it operated under the name of Bureau One and carried out the scorched earth policy in the face of advancing German troops. The section of this division responsible for the kidnappings and murders of the enemies of Communism is the notorious Section Nine, the section for terror and diversion.

Which brings us to SMERSH.

In his series of James Bond thrillers, the late Ian Fleming popularized SMERSH as "the official murder organization of the Soviet government." SMERSH is derived from the Russian, *smert shpionam,* or "death to spies," and actually did exist as an organization during World War II. It was originally established by the Cheka in 1921 to spy on the Russian military and ensure its loyalty. This special section was known as the Double-O Section (from which, no doubt, Ian Fleming got the idea to label James Bond as Agent 007, the Double-O meaning, in the fictional case, that he had "a license to kill"), and its members were infiltrated into every level of the Red Army. During World War II the Double-O Section was expanded throughout all the Soviet armed forces and redesignated as SMERSH. As such it took on the additional duties of intercepting enemy paratroopers and tracking down Russian deserters, and wherever the Red Army occupied foreign territory it was SMERSH's job to apprehend all German agents of the Abwehr (German Army Intelligence) and the Gestapo. In order to carry out these duties, SMERSH was given the power to hold summary courts-martial at the front and to execute those condemned to death for spying.

After World War II, SMERSH was dissolved and absorbed into the KGB machinery, where it remains today. But the fact that it no longer exists as a separate unit does not mean that its former functions are not carried out from time to time by carefully chosen individual agents, whenever the dictates of Soviet policy demand it. One such individual was Bogdan Stashinskiy.

Bogdan Stashinskiy, who defected to the West in 1961, was a Double-O agent; a trained assassin for the

KGB who did nothing but kill. Stashinskiy was not a spy in the strictest sense. He did not collect intelligence, or transmit it, or evaluate it. But he was an important member of an espionage organization which also functions as the enforcing arm of Soviet policy.

Stashinskiy got his start with the KGB almost by accident. No infraction is too small to escape the notice of the Soviet Secret Police, and when young Bogdan was arrested as a schoolboy for riding on a train without a ticket, it was a KGB officer who questioned him. At that time, as now, the Ukraine was the heartland of a burning nationalist movement, and all of Bogdan's family were members of an underground organization that favored Ukrainian independence from the Soviet Union. The KGB officer made a few veiled threats to Stashinskiy's family, and it was a measure of the man he was to become that the boy did not stand up long under this casual pressure. He quickly told the officer all he knew about the underground, and volunteered to supply information in the future. The information he supplied was good enough to earn him a job with the KGB Spetsgruppa, a gang of young toughs used by the Secret Police for strong-arm work.

For the next two years Stashinskiy was involved in the KGB drive to wipe out the last of the Ukrainian nationalist movement. It was rough-and-tumble work with more than its share of deception, disloyalty, beating, and torturing—the kind of work deliberately calculated to harden and dehumanize a young man. After two years of it Stashinskiy was ready for something bigger. He had never cared much for political ideology, but he convinced his superiors that he was a dedicated Communist and was sent to a KGB school in Kiev to prepare for a major assignment in the West. In Kiev, Stashinskiy studied Polish and German, and was trained in undercover technique. Then, equipped with a new identity under the name Josef Lehmann, he was posted to East Berlin to work for a Soviet delegation there. The work was routine and rather dull for someone used to the active life of the Spetsgruppa, but Stashinskiy did his job without complaint and waited for a more interesting assignment. It was soon to come. After he had been in East Berlin long enough to prove his dependability, he was summoned to KGB headquarters in the Karlshorst, relieved of his duties with the delegation, and given details of his new job. His mission: locate and assassinate two enemies of the Soviet Union, the exiled Ukrainian leaders Lev Rebet and Stepan Bandera.

The assassination order was part of Moscow's attempt to put an end to the still smoldering Ukrainian nationalist movement. Although the nationalists had no real organization within the Soviet Union, they maintained an active underground abroad, with headquarters in Munich, Germany. The nationalists were not so much a threat to the Kremlin as they were a political nuisance, a persistent irritation on the Russian body politic, and the KGB was given the job of scratching and eliminating the itch.

When Stashinskiy reported himself ready to undertake the mission, a Russian weapons expert was flown from

Moscow to East Berlin bearing the assassin's gun. It was an aluminum tube weighing less than eight ounces, just over six inches long and three quarters of an inch in diameter. Hermetically sealed to the tube was a plastic ampule containing a liquid poison. The poison, colorless and odorless, was ejected in a fine spray when the weapon was fired. Stashinskiy was told that for maximum results the poison should be fired directly into the victim's face at a range of no more than eighteen inches. The poisonous vapors would then be breathed in, and the arteries carrying blood to the brain would become paralyzed. Death would follow within ninety seconds, said the man from Moscow. He also assured Stashinskiy that long before an autopsy could be performed on the victim, the effect of the poison would wear off and leave no trace of the killing agent. It would then appear that the man had died from thrombosis.

It was a perfect murder weapon, but it involved some risk to the user of it. Stashinskiy was told that he would be safe—provided he kept his own head several inches away from the poisonous vapors. As a precaution he was given several tablets to take just before using the weapon. The tablets would protect him by enlarging the arteries, to permit an unimpeded flow of blood should he inhale a small amount of the poison. In addition, he was given a compress inhalant to clasp over his face if he felt he had inhaled too much. Thus equipped, Stashinskiy set out from Berlin for Munich.

His first victim, Lev Rebet, was an anti-Russian journalist who was a popular literary figure in the Ukrainian exile community in Munich. The KGB dossier described him as being powerfully built, with a shaven head. He was known to divide his time between two Ukrainian emigré offices in Munich. With this description Stashinskiy was able to spot his victim on his first day in Munich. For the next two days, using standard procedure, he followed Rebet to establish the pattern of the man's movements. On the morning of the third day he picked up Rebet as he was getting off a streetcar near his office. The assassin moved quickly into the office building ahead of his victim, the weapon rolled into a newspaper in his right hand. He began to climb the circular staircase ahead of Rebet. At the first-floor landing he turned; Rebet was a few steps below him. Without breaking stride, Stashinskiy started down the stairs again. As he passed Rebet he discharged the weapon directly into his face and continued downstairs without looking back. He heard Rebet stumble, but still, perfectly trained, he did not look back. He walked out of the building and went directly to the Koeglmuehlbach Canal a half mile away where he dropped the weapon into the water.

That night the Ukrainian emigré press reported that Lev Rebet had died, the victim of a natural heart attack.

The assassination of Stepan Bandera was a more complex operation, but was carried out with the same dispatch. Bandera, called "The Sly Fox," was the leading symbol of Ukrainian resistance, and was also secretly affiliated with several Western intelligence agencies. He was a difficult man to find and, with his training, even more difficult to follow, and Stashinskiy had to make four separate trips to Munich before he could establish a pattern of the man's movements. He finally found the apartment of the Ukrainian listed under the pseudonym "Poppel." After careful reconnaissance of the building he waited in the downstairs lobby at the hour in the late afternoon when the Ukrainian leader usually came home. As Bandera started up the steps, his arms burdened with groceries, Stashinskiy started down. Using the same procedure as he had with Rebet, he fired the weapon as he passed his victim, then continued down the steps without looking back. He walked to the same canal and disposed of his weapon. That night he was on his way back to Berlin with two successful assassinations to his credit.

He was never credited with any more. Shortly after the Bandera killing, Stashinskiy was convinced by his German girl friend—of whom the KGB sharply disapproved, for she had borne him an illegitimate son—to defect to the West. He brought with him one of the few authenticated accounts of KGB murder methods.

No account of Soviet intelligence activities would be complete without mention of the KGB's bitter rival, the Chief Intelligence Directorate of the General Staff of the Red Army, the Glavnoye Razvedyvatelnoye Upravlenie, or GRU. This military counterpart to the KGB is a worldwide intelligence apparatus in itself, but because it is subordinate to the Red Army it is less of a political force within the Soviet system than is the KGB. The operational procedures of the two agencies are similar; the essential difference is that the tasks of the GRU are mainly, although not exclusively, military.

When the American Central Intelligence Agency was formed in 1947 to coordinate all American intelligence activities, the Russians attempted to counter by doing the same. The GRU and KGB (then known as MGB) were merged into a single central agency known as the Committee of Information, or KI. The experiment was a failure; the inbred suspiciousness of rival Soviet bureaus doomed it from the start and the two organizations were again placed on a separate footing little more than a year later. Today they operate as theoretical equals, supposedly working in tandem but often pulling in opposite directions.

And, as we shall see, in the wonderland of Soviet politics where words have multiple meanings, the KGB is far more equal than its military neighbor.

2 THE PROFESSIONALS

Soviet intelligence overseas, whether it is KGB or GRU, operates to a great degree through a network of agents placed in its embassies, missions, and official agencies. In the jargon of the espionage world, these are "legal" operators—a somewhat misleading term. "Legal" operators have an official cover job and often have diplomatic immunity, but their duties as spies are certainly not legal. These "legal" agents under diplomatic cover—and enjoying diplomatic immunity—at the Soviet Embassy in Washington, and at the two Russian missions to the United Nations in New York, are able to operate free of the fear of arrest or imprisonment. If caught, the worst they can expect is to be ordered out of the country. This ease of operation extends to their working routine, since the information they gather can be transmitted to Moscow Center through normal diplomatic channels—coded messages and untouchable diplomatic pouches—and instructions from Center received in the same manner.

A Soviet "legal" operator in the United States is limited only by the travel restrictions placed on all Communist diplomats, and by the disquieting knowledge that he is likely to be under surveillance by the FBI. Despite these limitations, "legal" agents are able to operate with the knowledge that even so diligent an organization as the FBI cannot watch every Soviet diplomat, second secretary, typist, and chauffeur twenty-four hours a day. To do so would require far more manpower than the FBI has at its disposal. In addition, Russian agents in the United States do not have to move about much to perform their functions, since a great deal of data shipped from the United States comes from public sources such as magazines, government pamphlets, and technical publications. Despite this relative security, "legal" agents are often caught by standard counterespionage methods since their official positions expose them to scrutiny. In that sense they are far more vulnerable than the "illegals," the spies who have no official cover at all.

The "illegals" are the glamour boys of modern espionage, the highly trained agents who are inserted into an alien society much like a parachutist jumping behind

enemy lines during wartime. Unlike their "legal" counterparts, they must operate alone, often for years, away
from home and family and the use of their native language, and always with the knowledge that, if captured,
they can expect no help from their masters. The best
of the illegals are much like actors and artists, and
they take risks for reasons which are sometimes not
entirely clear to themselves or their fellowmen. In that
respect they seem to be motivated by the same dyna-
mism that makes men want to climb mountains or crack
speed records. The risk is part of their lives, the pressure unrelenting. These are the professionals. The best
of them operate brilliantly under this pressure; the
worst, when they crack, crack badly.

Richard Sorge was one of the best: a Russian agent
who has been called the most accomplished spy of the
twentieth century. For eight years, just before and
during World War II, Sorge operated an espionage ring
in Japan which supplied the Soviet Union with information so valuable that, literally, the course of history was
changed. He did this by penetrating into the very hearts
of both the Japanese cabinet and the German Embassy
in Tokyo at a time when the fate of the world was in
the balance. Because of the information he uncovered
there, Russia was able to throw back the German armies
from the gates of Moscow. In a very literal sense, Sorge
saved Russia from annihilation. His reward was a
Japanese hangman's noose, and the knowledge that
his country, in traditional espionage fashion, had disowned him.

A great spy must be a political animal, a man of the times in which he lives. He must be able to evaluate the information which comes into his hands in a political sense, and be able to gauge the social and economic importance of the intelligence he has gathered. Sorge was this type of spy: he made a sharp distinction between intelligence and mere information. Any spy can gather information about troop movements and gun emplacements. To Sorge, the absolute power of espionage lay in discovering the political intentions of the enemy. This was intelligence, and he left the tapping of wires and the pilfering of papers to lesser men. Sorge never rifled a safe or peeked through a keyhole: he never had to. He worked himself into such a position of confidence with both the Germans and the Japanese that any paper he wanted to see was shown to him openly. No doors were locked to him, no conversations considered too confidential for his ears. Simply by the style with which he operated, Sorge made other spies look like amateurs.

Richard Sorge was born in Russia in 1895, the son of a Russian mother and a German father who worked as an engineer in the Baku oil fields. He was a boy with two homelands, and was bilingual and bicultural. The family returned to Berlin before World War I, and Sorge at nineteen was called up to fight in the Kaiser's army. He fought in a student regiment through some of the worst battles in Flanders, and later was transferred to the Russian front. There he was wounded twice, the second wound giving him a permanent limp. He later described his life in those years as "a progress from the school chair to the slaughtering block," and claimed that it was the horrors of war that made him a Communist.

After the war he completed his studies in Berlin and became an ardent worker in the Communist cause. He was a young man of great talent and personality, and he made such an impression on local Communist leaders that his reputation traveled to Moscow. He was soon invited to visit Comintern headquarters there—a visit which was to last for two years. While he was in Moscow he was made a member of the Soviet Communist Party, a rare honor for a foreigner, and was offered the opportunity to work for Soviet intelligence. He was immediately attracted to the idea. Sorge was a man of action, and although he was politically oriented, routine Party activities bored him. He had no patience with Party ideologists whose greatest delight was an all-night hairsplitting discussion on the meaning of Karl Marx's dialectical materialism. Intelligence seemed like a way to translate politics into action, and when the offer was made he knew he had found his career.

After several years of traveling about Europe organizing local Communist Parties, Sorge was recalled to Moscow and transferred to the Fourth Bureau of the Red Army. The Fourth Bureau was in charge of military intelligence, and was the predecessor of the agency we now know as the GRU. At that time the Fourth Bureau was involved in setting up a worldwide intelligence network to rival that of the OGPU (later the KGB), and

Sorge was assigned to the Far East section. As a cover
for his work he returned to Germany and established
himself as a journalist. He did this without difficulty, for
he was a clever writer and an instinctive newspaperman.
He quickly developed a sound reputation and was given
several important assignments in China. He spent three
years there, mostly in Shanghai, and it was in China
that he formed the nucleus of his famous Tokyo spy
ring. His first recruit was a Japanese named Ozaki
Hotsumi who was also a journalist, and who had definite
leanings toward Communism. The second member of
the ring was a German, Max Klausen, who was a radio
operator and a former member of the Hamburg Communist Party. When Moscow Center ordered Sorge to
Japan, the two recruits went with him, Ozaki as second-
in-command and Klausen as the communications link.

In 1933 Sorge went to Tokyo as the Far East correspondent of the influential German newspaper *Frank-
furter Zeitung*. He also brought with him letters of
introduction to the German ambassador in Tokyo, and
once in Japan he had little difficulty in being received in
the highest diplomatic circles. The German community in
Tokyo accepted him at once on the basis of his introduc-
tions, his journalistic reputation, and his military service
in the German Army. He joined the Nazi Party in Japan,
and within a short time was on a friendly basis with
most of the officials at the German Embassy.

The secret of Sorge's success, as with most great
spies, was that as far as his personality was concerned he
did not try to be anything but what he was. He was

known in Tokyo as a brilliant, rather eccentric man of the world who was also a heavy drinker and a chaser after women. This was not a part he played; this was Richard Sorge. Men admired him, women adored him, and his bohemian habits were forgiven because of his talent and charm. Everyone who came in contact with him during those Tokyo days recognized something of the genius in Richard Sorge—and genius he must have been, for he was soon within the inner counsels of the German Embassy. His advice was sought by the naval attaché, by Prince Albrecht von Urach, by the ambassador himself.

Was there a mining concession in China gone wrong, or a ticklish problem in Siam? "Ask Sorge" was the usual solution to the problem, and Sorge never failed to come up with an intelligent, informed, and practical answer. His opinions carried so much weight that he was considered an unofficial member of the Embassy staff, and by 1936 he had ingratiated himself so thoroughly that he even had his own private room within the Embassy compound. He attended secret meetings whenever he wished, acted as unofficial secretary for the military attaché, Colonel Ott, and on certain occasions actually encoded messages destined for Berlin which were considered too secret to be entrusted to ordinary members of the staff. During that period Sorge managed to see every major document bearing on German-Japanese relations, as well as most of the secret messages sent by the Embassy to Berlin. Everything he saw, he recorded and sent on to Moscow Center.

While Sorge was mesmerizing the Germans, his second-in-command, Ozaki, was enjoying a similar success with the Japanese. Ozaki's reputation as an expert on China was such that he was soon accepted into the inner circle of advisers to the Japanese premier, Prince Konoye. Although he did not have Sorge's great personal charm, Ozaki had the advantage of working among his own countrymen, and his rise was as spectacular as his master's. By 1938 he, too, was in a position of confidence and was appointed consultant and special assistant to the secretary of the Japanese cabinet. Thus, between them, Sorge and Ozaki had access to the most secret documents of both the Japanese cabinet and the German Embassy. It was a formidable one-two punch.

The routine work of the ring was left to the subordinates. Sorge and Ozaki gathered the intelligence, and Max Klausen transmitted it to Moscow Center via a special shortwave station near Vladivostok. The two other members of the ring were a man named Branko Vukelic, who acted as a reserve radio operator, and a Japanese Communist named Miyagi Yotoku. The ring never numbered more than five, but special couriers were occasionally used to smuggle microfilm out of the country and across Siberia to Moscow.

World War II broke out in Europe in 1939, and by that time, on the other side of the world, Sorge's position at the German Embassy in Tokyo had become unassailable. His closest friend in Japan, the former military attaché Colonel Ott, had been appointed as the new ambassador, and now there was absolutely no document concerning the German war plans that Sorge did not see. And since Japan and Germany were allies, similar information was being given to the Japanese cabinet—where Ozaki was able to confirm and amplify the intelligence Sorge had gathered.

In 1941 Sorge sent to Moscow the single most important piece of intelligence he had yet uncovered. Sent urgently and personally by courier across Siberia, the document gave unmistakable evidence that German troops were being shifted to the Russian frontier, and that Hitler was about to break the German-Russian Non-Aggression Pact and attack the Soviet Union.

Strangely, Stalin received the report with skepticism. For a cold and ruthless man the Russian dictator had a rather naïve faith in his pact with Hitler; he was not prepared to face the facts. Sorge tried desperately to convince Stalin. He sent additional reports which gave the exact number and disposition of the German divisions, and in May he was able to report the exact date of the attack—June 22. Incredibly, Stalin's attitude remained unchanged. He either ignored Sorge's reports or minimized them, telling his advisers that all agents in the field tend to exaggerate.

On June 22 the Germans struck across the border with overwhelming force. The unprepared Russians suffered shattering losses and were forced to retreat toward Moscow, ceding huge chunks of territory to the Wehrmacht invaders. The night of the German attack Sorge sat in the home of one of his many Japanese girl friends, listening to the news on the radio. He wept uncontrollably. To the girl's hesitant questions he could only shake his head. There was nothing he could say to her, or to anyone else.

There were bitter recriminations within the Kremlin over Stalin's refusal to heed the warnings from Sorge; the Fourth Bureau, with the power of the Red Army behind it, was particularly biting in its attacks. But there was no time for saying "I told you so." Russia's western provinces were overrun, and her armies were collapsing daily before the rolling might of Hitler's panzer divisions. In this desperate situation the Kremlin leaders were faced with a decision which would not only affect the winning of the war, but might change the course of history. To help make this decision, they turned to Richard Sorge, the man whose advice they had once—to their now deep regret—ignored.

Japan was Germany's ally. Would she strike at Russia's Far Eastern Siberian frontier and involve the Red Army in a two-front war? The Russians kept a large standing army in the Far East, on the borders of embattled China and facing Japan, an army that was desperately needed for the defense of Moscow. But the Soviet leaders did not dare move a single man west to help oppose the Nazis until they were sure that Japan would not attack Siberia. That was the question they posed to Sorge: *What will Japan do?* Will she attack Siberia, or will she strike south toward Singapore and Indonesia against the British, the Dutch, and eventually the Americans?

It was a question which Sorge with all his brilliance

could not answer at once—simply because the Japanese, themselves, had not yet decided. He could guess, but he couldn't know. Early in July the Japanese Imperial Conference agreed on a general mobilization, but postponed a decision on which way to send the troops. But Sorge had the political instinct that all great spies must have, and he made his own shrewd analysis of the situation. If the Japanese attacked Siberia, he reasoned, they would be aiding an ally and winning a war, but if they struck to the south they stood to gain an oil-rich empire which they needed more than land or glory. He concluded that Japan would not attack Russia and so advised Moscow, but his unsupported opinion was not enough for Stalin. With German troops sweeping through the Ukraine and closing on Moscow, the Russian dictator waited for a confirmation of Sorge's analysis.

The confirmation came in August. As Sorge had forecast, the Japanese High Command decided not to go to war with the Soviet Union during 1941. Ozaki knew the decision almost as soon as it was made. Sorge flashed the word to Moscow at once, but Stalin again stubbornly demanded more proof, and it was not until October that Sorge was able to convince him that the Japanese would indeed strike to the south. This time, at last, he was believed. Stalin gave orders for the troops to be moved to the defense of Moscow. In the next two months the entire 16th Army, augmented by eleven rifle divisions, was transferred to the western front. The shift in the balance of forces was enough to save Moscow.

In this one evaluation of intelligence, Sorge had risen to the greatest heights of espionage. He had literally saved his country from destruction, and had influenced events far beyond his own lifetime; but now the sands were running out. The spy ring was already under suspicion by the Special Higher Police of Tokyo. Sorge felt it—the best ones always know when it is time to cut and run—but it was too late. Miyagi Yotoku, the least important member of the ring, was arrested. During his interrogation Miyagi threw himself out of the second-floor window of the police station. Intending to kill himself, he fell into a tree and broke his leg. Taken back into the station, under torture he broke down and named the other members of the ring.

When Sorge was arrested he had no option but to confess. The Japanese knew everything by now, and he was confident that in view of his brilliance as a spy the Soviet Union would help him in some way. After all, he had saved Mother Russia, and he was sure that Stalin would manage to have him exchanged for prisoners of war or other captured spies. His confidence was misplaced; Stalin did not lift a finger to save him. Both Sorge and Ozaki were hanged.

Rudolf Abel was another professional who operated at his best when under pressure. Sorge's field was wartime Japan, Abel's was peacetime America, but the pressures on the two men were the same. The lonely life, the constant fear of detection, the ever present shadow of the gallows: these are the pressures that mold a spy and make him what he is. In Abel's case the result was a brilliant agent. In the case of his assistant, Reino Hayhanen, the result was a broken man.

Rudolf Ivanovich Abel was an intelligence officer of long standing when he was assigned to head the KGB operations in the United States. Behind him was a distinguished career during World War II as a Soviet spy operating in German-occupied Russia. His most notable feat during that time was the penetration of the headquarters of the German High Intelligence, the Abwehr, and after that his stock rose quickly in the KGB. After the war he served both in France and in England, and eventually was sent to New York as the KGB's illegal *rezident* in the United States. (In Soviet intelligence the *rezident* is the agent in the field who controls the operation against a particular country. The network he controls is called the *rezidentura*.) When he came to New York, Abel was in his middle forties, married, and the father of two children. Rather than being a hindrance, this family status was an important qualification for his work, for high-level *rezidents* are almost always required to leave hostages at home in case they are ever tempted to defect to the other side.

Part of Abel's orders was to have no connection with the Soviet Embassy in the United States, nor with any clandestine Russian agency operating there. Because of this, he was told to find his own way into the United States, and the only assistance that Moscow Center gave him consisted of a number of false documents describing him as a displaced person of German-Irish descent. Because Canadian immigration regulations are far less strict than those of the United States, Abel applied to Ottawa for a Canadian immigration permit. It was granted. He arrived in 1947 and remained in Canada for several months before slipping over the border into the United States. Once there, he was on station and ready to operate.

During his first year in America, Abel took no part in actual espionage activities; following prescribed KGB routine, he concentrated on establishing his network. For a cover, he took the name of Emil Goldfus and the occupation of an artist. He was not a particularly brilliant painter, but he could paint well enough and knew enough about art to be able to gather a set of artists and bohemian types about him in a short time. The cover occupation was not chosen casually, for as an artist he could disappear whenever he wished, keep odd hours, and indulge in other unconventional behavior without arousing comment. He rented a studio in a dilapidated section of Brooklyn and there, in the next years, was almost always surrounded by a noisy circle of friends. He seemed to love company, and it was only on certain nights of the week, always at ten o'clock, that he would announce that he wanted to be alone. Carefully bolting the doors behind his departing friends, he would sweep away a pile of tattered canvases and extract a radio transmitter powerful enough to put him in direct contact with Moscow Center. For the next thirty minutes he would be absorbed in tapping out high-speed code transmissions.

The information which Abel's network collected, and which was sent home by the *rezident* in this fashion from his apartment and elsewhere, was more than enough to satisfy the high standards of Moscow Center, both as to quality and quantity. In fact, the volume of information which Abel produced was so great after only one year of operation that he soon needed an assistant. The man sent by Center to help him was Konon Molody, an old friend and associate. We shall meet Molody again in this narrative, in another country and under another name—but for now he is Molody. He stayed with Abel for almost five years, and the two men worked together perfectly.

Then Molody was sent off on another assignment, and Center replaced him with Reino Hayhanen. One of the more persistent myths about Soviet intelligence is that the system consistently produces high-quality agents capable of performing their duties rigidly and without question. Reino Hayhanen was a case to disprove the myth.

Hayhanen was inserted into the United States as an illegal in true KGB fashion, assuming the name of an American-born laborer, Eugene Nicolai Maki. The real Maki was born in Enaville, Idaho, in 1919, the son of an American mother and a Finnish immigrant father. Several years after he was born, Maki's parents sailed with him for Estonia, and the three dropped from sight, presumably lost in the carnage of World War II.

Posing as Maki, Hayhanen, who spoke fluent Finnish, lived in Finland for several years under orders from the

KGB. He was carefully schooled in his role as Maki, and in 1951 he presented himself at the American legation in Helsinki and showed a birth certificate indicating that he was, indeed, Eugene Maki born in Enaville, Idaho, in 1919. A year later, after a routine investigation by U.S. authorities, he was given an American passport; after a last-minute trip to Moscow for instructions, he sailed for New York on the *Queen Mary*. It was not until 1954, after two years of lying low and perfecting his role as Maki, that Hayhanen was assigned to Abel as deputy American *rezident*.

What followed was a burlesque of the normally rigid KGB operational procedures. Upon meeting his new assistant, Abel was shocked to find that Hayhanen had not only forgotten most of his training in codes, but that his ideas about security were so elementary that he constituted a danger to the entire network. The *rezident* complained at once to Center. In a popular novel about espionage, the guilty Hayhanen would have been recalled to Moscow for a refresher course at hard labor. In actuality, Center simply told Abel to stop complaining and to make the best of a bad situation. This he did, unhappily. By this time Abel had been working in the field for six years under heavy pressure, and when Center instructed him to return to Moscow for six months' leave he went gratefully, though with considerable misgivings about leaving his new deputy in charge.

When Abel returned to New York in 1956, he found to his horror that Hayhanen had broken every rule of security possible. During all the time that the boss was away, the deputy *rezident* had operated his radio transmitter from the same location instead of moving it from place to place. In addition, he had let the network go to seed by failing periodically to collect information from the agents in the field. Worst of all, he had blown his cover, closing the machine shop he was supposed to be operating and living squalidly in a room behind the shop. There Abel found him, surrounded by empty whiskey bottles and well on his way to total alcoholism.

This was too much for Center. Once again, in the world of fiction an agent from SMERSH would have been dispatched to put an end to the bumbling career of Reino Hayhanen. Instead, he was simply ordered home, sailing for Le Havre on the *Liberté* in April 1957. Once in Paris, he dutifully followed Abel's instructions and had several meetings with Soviet agents, who then instructed him to fly to West Berlin and then on to Moscow. To remove any suspicions he might have, Hayhanen was told that he had been promoted in rank to major in the KGB and was given three hundred dollars to cover his expenses.

But, somehow, through the drunken haze in which he lived, Hayhanen saw the handwriting on the wall. He realized that what awaited him in Moscow was not glory but an escort to Siberia. After careful thought he telephoned the American Embassy in Paris. Two days later he defected to the CIA station there. He was returned to the United States for a long, personal interview with Allen Dulles, then head of the CIA, and eventually placed in the custody of the FBI.

The responsibilities and limitations of the Federal

Bureau of Investigation are strictly defined in laws enacted by Congress. These laws encompass some 170 federal investigative matters, ranging from bank robbery and kidnapping to sabotage and treason. One of the functions of the organization is internal counterespionage, and in the performance of this duty the FBI is somewhat the domestic counterpart of the CIA, whose operations are limited by law to areas outside the United States. As we shall see later, both agencies tend to bend or break these limitations when it suits their needs. A further difference between the two agencies is that while the CIA strives for anonymity, the FBI is publicity-conscious to an extreme. Bureau agents address Kiwanis, Rotarian, and Chamber of Commerce meetings regularly, and the FBI itself, through its well-known director, J. Edgar Hoover, encourages the production of books and motion pictures glorifying the agency. Thus it was not surprising that Hoover later claimed to have "smashed the Soviet espionage operations of Colonel Rudolf Ivanovich Abel," although if Hayhanen had not defected to the CIA, Abel might have gone undetected indefinitely.

Once in American hands, Hayhanen was more than happy to give his captors all the details he knew of KGB operational procedure. He even gave them the locations of certain of his "dead drops," an intelligence term for hiding places where messages can be left for other agents. One of these "dead drops" was a hole in a flight of concrete steps in Brooklyn's Prospect Park. FBI agents found that the hole had been filled in, but after digging away they discovered a bolt about two inches long. The bolt was perfectly ordinary-looking, save that it had been hollowed out and contained a typewritten message. The message had been meant for Hayhanen, and no one familiar with the ineptitude of the deputy *rezident* would have been surprised by the contents. It read: "Nobody came to meeting either 8th or 9th as I was advised I should. Why? Should he be inside or outside? Is time wrong? Place seems right. Please check."

When told about the hollow bolt, Hayhanen amiably provided further information. "We used all kinds of holowed-out things," he told the agents. "We had hollow pens and pencils, screws, batteries, and coins."

The word "coins" struck a response with the interviewing agents, for the FBI had come into the possession of a hollow Jefferson nickel several years before. The coin had been cleverly made from two different nickels, and in the letter "R" of the word "TRUST" (of "IN GOD WE TRUST") a tiny hole had been drilled so that a small instrument could be used to snap open the device. Inside the coin was a microphotograph of ten columns of typewritten numbers, five digits in each number and twenty-one numbers in most of the columns. Efforts to break the code had been unsuccessful, and the coin and the photo had been gathering dust in the FBI files ever since. When they were shown to Hayhanen, he happily agreed that the message had been meant for him; the coin had gone astray. Although his knowledge of the code was rusty, he was able to interpret enough of the key groups to allow decoding of the message. It had been sent directly from Moscow Center, and was an odd mixture of espionage business and news from home:

1. We congratulate you on a safe arrival. We confirm the receipt of your letter to the address "V" repeat "V" and the reading of letter Number 1.

2. For organization of cover, we gave instructions to transmit to you three thousand in local currency. Consult with us prior to investing this in any business, advising the character of this business.

3. According to your request, we will transmit the formula for the preparation of soft film and news separately, together with your mother's letter.

4. It is too early to send you the GAMMAS [one-time pads used for enciphering]. Encipher short letters, but the longer ones make with insertions. All the data about yourself, place of work, address, etc. must not be transmitted in one cipher message. Transmit insertions separately.

5. The package was delivered to your wife personally. Everything is all right with the family. We wish you success. Greetings from the comrades. Number 1, 3rd of December.

In all of his dealings with Hayhanen, Colonel Abel had observed standard security precautions. He was known to his subordinate only by the cover name of "Mark," and all meetings between the two men had taken place on neutral ground, places which could not be traced to either of them. All meetings, that is, except one, and it was this mild breach of security which led to Abel's arrest. On one occasion he had had to question Hayhanen closely concerning some material he had produced. Because the questioning might take some time, the usually cautious Abel chose as a meeting place a storeroom which he had rented away from his studio. Under relentless questioning by FBI agents, Hayhanen was able to recall hazily that the storeroom was somewhere near Clark and Fulton streets in Brooklyn. A lengthy search of that area showed that such a store-room had been rented to a man named Emil Goldfus, who had given the landlord his home address. This was Abel's only other lapse from tight security. According to KGB procedure, he should have rented the studio in another name and given a false address. Two small deviations from security, but they were enough.

When FBI agents called at the studio they were told that Goldfus was out of town, and for good reason. When Hayhanen had failed to arrive in Moscow, KGB Center had warned Abel, ordering him to leave New York at once. He was told to lie low in Florida and await further instructions. Then, inexplicably, after two months he was ordered back to New York. Again, under storybook conditions, the valuable Abel with his cover jeopardized would have been recalled to Moscow and a new *rezident* inserted. Instead, KGB Center ordered one of their top agents back to New York to almost certain capture.

On his arrival in New York, Rudolf Abel was arrested by the FBI on charges of illegal entry into the United States. He was brought to trial on October 14, 1957, on charges of conspiring to obtain military secrets, in addition to the illegal entry charge. At first Abel refused to answer any questions put to him; eventually he admitted his name and the fact that he was a Russian citizen, although he denied engaging in espionage. This was in accordance with KGB procedure. All Soviet agents are instructed in the intricacies of the laws of the countries in which they are to operate. Agents working in the United States know that, if captured, they face a possible death penalty. Accordingly, they are trained to deny all charges and to refuse to make any statements. In Great Britain, by contrast, where there is no death penalty for peacetime espionage, agents are permitted by Center to divulge all information short of actual confession in the hopes of buying a shorter prison term.

Rudolf Abel was provided by the State with the best defense attorney available, the distinguished lawyer James Donovan, but the weight of evidence was too strong and he was found guilty as charged. During the period before sentence was pronounced, Donovan addressed an appeal for clemency to the presiding judge. In it he said, prophetically: "Who knows but that at some later date an American might not fall into Russian hands charged with similar offenses? If Colonel Abel is then still alive, maybe it will be possible to effect an exchange of prisoners."

The judge took note of this argument and sentenced Abel to thirty years' imprisonment. The U-2 incident was three years in the future, but Donovan's appeal and the judge's clemency helped set the scene that took place that misty February morning on Berlin's Glienicker Bridge.

Six months after the exchange, by midsummer of 1962, it was common diplomatic knowledge that Colonel Rudolf Ivanovich Abel had been placed in charge of the American desk at KGB Center in Moscow. Far from being punished for having been caught, Abel had been promoted into control of the KGB's most important overseas operation.

3 THE TALENTED AMATEURS

If this or any other account of modern espionage appears to pay particular attention to Soviet agents—making the story one of Russian spies versus American counterspies—there are two main reasons.

The first has to do with the nature of espionage itself and the difference between Western democracy and Eastern Communism. Normally, the KGB, the CIA, MI6, and their curious Chinese equivalent, the Social Affairs Department in Peking, do not advertise either their successes or their failures. There are exceptions, of course, and those exceptions give us most of our knowledge and information. Most of these exceptions are Communist spies caught by Western nations. For one thing, in the Western democracies it is often very difficult to hide from public scrutiny an event or a story that might be front-page news. For another, when an American or English spy is caught in the Soviet Union, little fuss is made beyond that which can exploit the immediate propaganda value. There is no pressure on Russian officials publicly to explain their methods used in catching spies, or how those spies infiltrated in the first place. And the officials themselves seem to take it more for granted: it's part of the game, they are older at it than we are, and more blasé.

The second reason is an odd one. It is because the Soviet Union has been so well served not only by professionals such as Richard Sorge and Rudolf Abel, but also by a host of talented amateurs. These are the scientists and technicians, none of them Russian but all of them intellectual adherents of Communism, who over the years have placed their talents at the disposal of the Kremlin. Although they were not so skilled at the espionage game as the professionals, with time they proved themselves to be no less effective.

This was a new breed of spy, born out of the despair of the economic Depression of the nineteen thirties, and out of the chaos of Hitler's Europe. For them the word traitor was meaningless; ideology was more important than patriotism. The new breed of spy was almost always an educated, sensitive person who recoiled with horror from the terrors of Nazism on one hand, and from the breadlines and soup kitchens on the other. In

the nineteen thirties, Communism seemed the only anti-
dote to both these evils, and many a liberal scientist
became a Communist for lack of a viable alternative.
From these ranks came the nuclear spies: the men who
stole the secret of the atomic bomb for Russia.

The development of the atomic bomb during World
War II was a highly guarded project run by teams of
American and British scientists. In America it was
known by the code name "Manhattan Project"; in England it was "Tube Alloys." In both countries the security surrounding the project was intense, for by 1943 it
had become clear that the race against time would be
won; that the bomb would be developed in time to
affect the outcome of the war. Equally important was the
knowledge that possession of the bomb would also affect the balance of power in the postwar years. Communism and Western democracy were in uneasy alliance
against Hitler at the time, but neither England nor
America felt that the Russians should share in the secrets of the nuclear weapons. Too much was at stake
for them in the postwar years to risk having the Soviet
Union as an atomic power. Accordingly, the Manhattan
and Tube Alloys projects were guarded as carefully from
the Russians as they were from the Germans and the
Japanese. The project was completed, the bomb was
tested, and when the holocaust that descended on Hiroshima and Nagasaki ended World War II, the Western
leaders congratulated themselves on having maintained the best-kept secret of the war. Then a twenty-
six-year-old Russian cipher clerk named Gouzenko

walked out of the Soviet Embassy in Ottawa with a load of confidential documents that showed how wrong those leaders had been. The Russians had stolen us blind.

Igor Gouzenko had a hard time defecting: nobody wanted him. This was 1945 and the Western democracies had little experience with political defectors. Today if a Communist diplomat wants to defect he simply calls the nearest office of the CIA or the FBI and says, in effect, "All right, I'm ready. Come and get me." Twenty-four hours later he will be eating bacon and eggs in the CIA cafeteria at Langley, Virginia, and prodding the duty officer about the size of his pension check. But in 1945, Gouzenko, hat in hand and with his shirt stuffed with confidential papers, had to go several times to the police, to a local newspaper, and even to the Prime Minister of Canada before anyone would take him seriously.

The Prime Minister was no help: he directed his staff to send the young man back to the Russian Embassy. Gouzenko had already tried offering the papers to the Ottawa *Journal,* but the editors there were unimpressed with the scoop of the century. He then had tried the police, but after scratching their heads, those worthies had decided that there was nothing much they could do to help the nice young Russian chap. He seemed rather nervous and upset, they agreed, but then all those foreigners were a bit odd.

When the Prime Minister refused to see him, Gouzenko panicked. As a member of the GRU he knew all about the long arm of the *sosedi*—"the neighbors"—as the

KGB is called by its sister service. He also knew that his GRU boss, Colonel Zabotin, was combing Ottawa for him and had placed a watch on his apartment. The code clerk was walking around with one hundred and nine top-secret Russian documents concealed under his shirt, and he had no illusions about his fate if Colonel Zabotin, who was built like the proverbial Russian bear, laid hands on him.

In desperation, Gouzenko appealed to his next-door neighbor, a sergeant in the Royal Canadian Air Force named Main. Sergeant Main found Gouzenko's story incredible, but the young Russian was so obviously terrified that he agreed to let him sleep in his flat that night. But the Canadian's disbelief vanished during the night when Zabotin and a crew of strong-arm men from the Embassy broke in Gouzenko's door and began to search the apartment. Watching from across the hall, Main realized that Gouzenko's life was really in danger, and he called the police. The attempted burglary was the worst move the Russians could have made, for now, at last, the Canadian authorities decided to take Gouzenko seriously. He was placed under the protection of the Royal Canadian Mounted Police, and the documents he had brought with him were examined carefully. Once they were translated, and analyzed, and finally understood, those papers started a sizzling train of fire that led from one espionage sensation to another. Before the fire was out, the Americans and the British were to realize exactly how much damage had been done by Russia's talented amateur spies.

Among the papers that Gouzenko took from the files of the Soviet Embassy was this telegram from Colonel Zabotin to Moscow Center:

31.7.45
To the Director.
We have worked out the conditions for a meeting with Alek in London. Alek will work in King's College, Strand. It will be possible to find him there through the telephone book. Meetings: October 7, 17, 27 on the street in front of the British Museum. The time, eleven o'clock in the evening. Identification sign: a newspaper under the left arm. Password: Best regards to Mikel. He cannot remain in Canada. At the beginning of September he must fly to London. Before his departure he will go to the Uranium Plant in Petawawa district where he will be for about two weeks. He promised, if possible, to meet us before his departure. He said he must come next year for a month to Canada. We handed over 500 dollars to him.

"Alek" was the Russian code name for Alan Nunn May, an experimental physicist who was a member of the British atomic team working in Canada. Nunn May was typical of the new breed of spy. He came to maturity in the nineteen thirties, fleeing from the twin specters of fascism and the depression straight into the waiting arms of the Kremlin. He was one of those scientists whose consciences were outraged by the British and American refusal to share atomic secrets with Russia. He preferred to ignore the fact that the Soviet Union had never collaborated with her Western allies, and that if Russia had developed the bomb first she would have guarded it just as jealously. Stalin never would have released the secret of the bomb to his allies, nor would Nunn May have expected him to. The Englishman later justified his actions on humanitarian grounds, but Nunn May was not a humanitarian, he was simply a good Communist. On humanitarian grounds, his attitude was nonsensical; from the Communist point of view it made a good deal of sense indeed.

Nunn May was never solicited by Soviet intelligence. He volunteered his services to the Soviet Embassy in Ottawa in 1945, bringing with him several samples of separated uranium isotopes. The uranium was handed over to Colonel Zabotin, who, as GRU chief in Ottawa, was responsible for the Canadian network. Zabotin considered the samples so important that he had them flown to Moscow on a special plane. He then made arrangements with Nunn May for further information to be passed, and offered the Englishman payment for his services. Nunn May refused. He insisted that he was spying not for money but for the good of the world. Zabotin insisted, knowing that payment would give him future leverage against Nunn May, and eventually the physicist took the money, plus two bottles of whiskey, as a sign of his subservience to the network.

By the time Nunn May returned to London in 1945, he was known to British counterintelligence, the MI5, as the man called "Alek" in the Gouzenko papers. He was kept under surveillance by MI5 for over a year in the hopes that he would lead them to other members of the ring. But Nunn May was apparently a lone operator, and in 1946 he was finally arrested by the Special

Branch of Scotland Yard and charged under the Official Secrets Act. Under questioning by Commander Burt of the Special Branch he admitted his actions, saying: "The whole affair was extremely painful to me, and I only embarked upon it because I felt this was a contribution I could make to the safety of mankind. I certainly did not do it for gain."

He was sentenced to ten years of penal servitude. He served six and a half years, and on his release was still convinced that he had acted for the best of motives. He returned to scientific work, and in 1962 was appointed professor of physics at the University of Ghana.

Alan Nunn May provided the Russians with several samples of uranium and the results of his experiments in atomic physics. There is no doubt that what he gave them was valuable, but it was insignificant when compared with the information passed by Dr. Klaus Fuchs. If there is a hierarchy among Soviet spies, Fuchs must rank just below Richard Sorge as the second most important agent of the century, for the German-born physicist gave the Russians the complete and detailed plans for the construction of the atomic bomb. There is little doubt that Soviet scientists would have developed the bomb on their own, but by conservative estimates Fuchs saved them two years of intensive research and experimentation. Some estimates run as high as ten years. More important than the actual years involved, Fuchs gave the Russians in 1949 an immediate atomic parity with the Americans and the British, thus altering the balance of power in the world.

The more we study Klaus Fuchs, the more we see the classic picture of the disillusioned liberal who turned to Communism as an answer to all the world's ills. He was born in Germany in 1911, the son of a highly respected Lutheran pastor. The young Fuchs was a prodigy, and at an early age was recognized as a brilliant physicist and mathematician. After Hitler seized power in Germany, Fuchs turned Communist and at once came into conflict with the Nazis. He was beaten up by Nazi thugs several times, and after the last such beating he fled from Germany to England. For the next six years, until the outbreak of World War II, he distinguished himself in his studies at Bristol and Edinburgh universities.

Fuchs was still a German citizen when the war began, theoretically an enemy alien, and in 1940 he was deported to an internment camp in Canada. His companions there were a mixed bag: most were fanatical followers of Hitler, but there was also a hard core of anti-Nazi Communists led by Hans Kahle. Fuchs gravitated naturally to the latter group and became friendly with Kahle, who is generally supposed to have been a Soviet intelligence agent. Were the seeds of espionage sown in that bleak Canadian camp? Fuchs has always denied it, denying also that Kahle influenced him in any way to spy for Russia. Whether he did or not, six months later Fuchs was out of the camp and back in England. Trained scientists of his ability were rare and valuable to England, and Fuchs was needed for the new Tube Alloys Project which was then being set up at Birmingham University by Professor Rudolf Peierls.

Fuchs was put to work on the atomic bomb project even though he was known to be a Communist—for by 1941 Russia had become England's ally, and it was people with fascist connections, rather than Communists, who were considered security risks at the time. The need for trained scientists was desperate, and Fuchs was involved at once in the most secret of assignments. All that was asked of him in advance was that he sign the Official Secrets Act and take out British naturalization papers. He did both cheerfully, swearing allegiance to the King.

Like Alan Nunn May, he did not wait to be approached by Soviet intelligence agents. As soon as he was cleared for secret work he got in touch with the GRU legal *rezident* in London, Semion Kremer, who operated under the cover of secretary to the Soviet military attaché. Fuchs and Kremer held several preliminary meetings in a private house not far from the Russian Embassy in Kensington Palace Gardens. Then, with procedure established, they settled down to business.

Throughout the rest of that year, and all of the following year, Fuchs passed carbon copies of his monthly reports either to Kremer or, when that was not practical, to a courier in Banbury. In these reports he covered the progress that British scientists were making toward development of the atomic bomb, and he did so at a time when elaborate security precautions in the United States were working against exactly such a leak occurring.

In December 1943, Fuchs was selected to join a team

of British scientists which was to go to the United States to work with the Americans on the final stages of the bomb. He thus would pass under the control of a different Soviet intelligence network—a KGB net in this case—and was given instructions for making contact with the *sosedi* in New York.

If the instructions sounded a bit ludicrous, it should be remembered that the Russians are long on detail and more than a bit theatrical in these matters. Life, it would seem, sometimes copies Hollywood. Fuchs was to be on a certain street corner on the Lower East Side of Manhattan at a certain time. He was to meet a man called "Raymond" who would be wearing a pair of gloves and carrying an additional pair of gloves as well. Raymond would also be carrying a green book. Fuchs was to be carrying a tennis ball. The rendezvous was carried out in January 1944, with Fuchs feeling more than a little absurd clutching a tennis ball in near-freezing weather.

Raymond—or, to give him his proper name, Harry Gold—was to be Fuchs' only contact in America. Gold was part of an elaborate network run by Anatoli Yakovlev, Rudolf Abel's predecessor as KGB *rezident* in New York. In addition to being in charge of all American operations, Yakovlev was responsible for all atomic espionage in the Western Hemisphere, and in that sense was in control of the GRU's Canadian network through Zabotin in Ottawa. To Yakovlev must go a major share of the credit for the success of Russia's nuclear espionage.

Fuchs had several meetings with Harry Gold in New York, passing information each time they met. Then the

physicist was ordered to report to Los Alamos, New
Mexico, for the final stage of construction and testing of
the first atomic bomb. Fuchs left promptly with the rest of
the British party. Amazingly, he did not inform Gold.
When he failed to appear at his next two scheduled
meetings, Gold reported the disappearance to Yakovlev.
Frantic efforts were made to find the vanished Fuchs,
but it was not until January 1945 that he was located
visiting his sister in Massachusetts. His explanation for
his disappearance was so fantastic that at first the Russians refused to swallow it, but they did not understand
the pedantic Fuchs, whose mind worked in strange channels. He had chosen not to tell the Russians where he
was going, he explained, because he had been warned
by the Americans that the Los Alamos location was considered *top secret!*

But this strict adherence to rules did not mean that
Fuchs was out of the espionage business. Indeed, Gold
found him to be just as forthcoming with information as
before his disappearance. Fuchs gave the cut-out a
verbal description of what progress had been made on
the bomb during 1944, and made arrangements for a
meeting in June at which he promised to deliver written
details. The meeting took place at the Castillo Bridge in
Santa Fe on June 2. Klaus Fuchs gave Harry Gold a
large sheaf of papers which contained every detail
known to him of the theory and construction of America's first atomic bomb. He also told Gold that great
progress had been made at Los Alamos, and that the
test explosion would take place in the Alamogordo Des-

ert in July. He was well aware of what he was doing; he was giving Russia the atomic bomb.

The two men parted at the Castillo Bridge, Fuchs to return to Los Alamos and Gold to take a bus to Albuquerque. On that bus, Harry Gold rolls out of our narrative, but only for the moment. Gold was on his way to keep an appointment with another amateur spy, David Greenglass, whom we soon shall meet.

At the end of the war Klaus Fuchs returned to England to an excellent job as head of the theoretical division of the British Atomic Energy Center at Harwell. The next three years were happy ones for him. His work at Harwell was fascinating and he saw it as his life's work. In addition, after his wartime fling, he was pretty much out of the espionage game. He maintained contact with the London network of Soviet intelligence, but at that time the Russians were primarily interested in the new American hydrogen bomb which had just been tested in the Pacific. Fuchs could tell them nothing about this; he was a stranger now to the American nuclear scene. The Russians recognized his potential value, however, and to bind him to the network they insisted for the first time that he accept a payment of £100 for "expenses." Like Nunn May, Fuchs refused. Like Nunn May, he finally accepted the money when it was explained, with startling candor, that it was a symbol which bound him to the cause.

In 1949 the Russians exploded their first atomic bomb. It must have been a cause of great pride for Fuchs, who had made it all possible, but that mushroom cloud over the Siberian wastelands also signaled the beginning of the end for him. The Russian triumph was a political, as well as an atomic, bomb. American authorities had been convinced that Russia was four to five years away from a test explosion. It seemed impossible to them that Russian technology could have closed the gap. Then a Soviet delegate to a meeting of the United Nations Atomic Energy Commission blundered when, in a boastful tirade, he let it be known that Russia had access to secrets which the United States had thought to be perfectly safe. The obvious answer was espionage, and the hunt was on.

By this time Nunn May had been tried and imprisoned, and it was clear from the start that this information could not have come from him. A bigger fish was wanted, someone who had been privy to all the details of the working of the bomb. By a process of elimination, the FBI narrowed down their search to three possible men. One of them was Fuchs.

The FBI information on Fuchs was placed in the hands of Britain's counterintelligence agency, the MI5. The security officers there proceeded slowly, for they were faced with a twofold problem: not only was Fuchs an important man at Harwell and one to be approached cautiously, but the evidence against him was very slight and MI5 was not at all sure of his guilt. The matter was finally dealt with by putting it in the hands of one of MI5's most skillful investigators, William Skardon. With his appointment the emphasis of this story shifts from espionage to counterintelligence. The spy had done his job; now it was the turn of the counter-spy.

William Skardon was a specialist in counterintelli-gence. He was the man used by MI5 to confront and break a special category of high-level traitors. To do this he needed tact, patience, and above all, the ability to sympathize with the man who was the object of his investigation. He had to get inside the suspect's mind; he had to find out what motivated a man to make him turn traitor. Skardon's suspects were all sensitive, intel-ligent men, and he had to conduct his investigations on an appropriate plane—no bullying tactics, no heavy-handed moralizing. In short, he had to be a combina-tion of psychiatrist and big brother to the men he was trying to hang. To all these abilities, Skardon was able to add one more. He was, as the Soviet agent Kim Philby later described him, "unquestionably the trick-iest cross-examiner I have met."

It was about this time that Fuchs began to have seri-ous doubts about what he had done. He was unsettled by the aggressive stance of the Soviet Union in the post-war years, and as he later said, "I came to the point when I knew that I disapproved of many actions of the Russian government and the Communist Party." These doubts increased as he watched the Soviet Union swallow coun-try after country in Eastern Europe. In addition, his conscience was troubled by the effect his great betrayal might have on his fellow nuclear scientists, some of whom had become his close friends. These doubts came close to unbalancing him, and he found himself indulging in a form of controlled schizophrenia, dividing his mind into two compartments: one for the world of Communism and espionage, the other for the world of his beloved Harwell and the scientists who worked with him there.

Fuchs was nervously walking this emotional tightrope when Skardon came on the scene. He told Fuchs frankly what was the purpose of his visit. The man from MI5 realized at once that Fuchs was troubled and upset. After their first few meetings Skardon also realized that the best way to handle the worried, conscience-stricken physicist was not to build up a secret case against him but, rather, to get him to confess. There was of course some danger in the plan. It would take time and Fuchs now knew that he was under suspicion. It was quite possible that he would try to flee England, or even (as had happened in similar cases) commit suicide. Skardon's associates at MI5 favored taking Fuchs into custody on some manufactured pretext before it was too late, but the specialist knew his man. He gambled on Fuch's love for his work at Harwell and his personal attachment to the scientists under him. He decided that Fuchs would not run.

Then began a series of meetings between Fuchs and Skardon which remain a classic example of the subtlety and patience required of a good counterintelligence agent. Skardon encouraged Fuchs to talk about his life, and Fuchs obliged. During those long meetings he talked about his hatred of the Nazis, about his underground days in Berlin, about his father, about his work at Harwell and how important it was. Over and over again he repeated how important his work was, and that it had to continue. Skardon always agreed. By this time the two men had reached that odd point which often exists between hunter and hunted: the point where they are no longer enemies, and each man trusts the other although both know that one will be destroyed before the business is over. Fuchs wanted to talk to Skardon, needed to talk to him, but he could never get himself to the point of confession. And then a casual remark by Skardon broke him.

They were having a quiet lunch at Abingdon after an all-morning session which had proved to be as fruitless as all the others. Fuchs had talked, but once again only of the Nazis, of Berlin, and of Harwell, always Harwell. Over lunch the two men agreed to suspend the interrogation and talk of something else. Skardon casually mentioned the departure from Harwell of Professor Skinner, who had been the number two man at the Center, just above Fuchs. He asked Fuchs if he knew who would be getting Skinner's job.

"Possibly me," Fuchs said cautiously. The question puzzled him since he was in line for the job through normal promotion.

Skardon said nothing, but he smiled slightly and shook his head. The meaning was clear. There was no likelihood of Fuchs ever being promoted into a higher position at Harwell now, whether he confessed or not. Fuchs thought for a moment, then stood up abruptly and asked to go back to his office. He was ready to confess. With promotion at Harwell closed to him there was no reason not to.

Fuchs was arrested by Commander Burt of the Special Branch of Scotland Yard, and charged with violating the Official Secrets Act. He could not be charged with treason, which carries the death penalty, because he had not given information to an enemy, but to an ally. He was given the maximum penalty of fourteen years, and served the full term in Wakefield Prison. When he was released he went directly to East Germany where he became Deputy Director of the East German Central Institute for Nuclear Physics at Rossendorf.

The bus carrying Harry Gold from Santa Fe to Albuquerque rolls back into our story here, and it rolls back carrying a very unhappy spy. Gold liked to think of himself as a professional, not a Moscow-trained professional to be sure, but he had been spying for the Russians for almost ten years and he had developed standards of his own. He had also developed a precise sense of exactly how far he could go in taking risks, and as he stared moodily out the bus window at the flat New Mexico landscape, he knew that he was about to go well over the line. Gold was a cut-out, an intermediary who picked up intelligence from an agent and delivered it to the *rezident*. That way the agent never saw the *rezident*, and could never identify him. This was basic security. But, Gold reflected, it was also basic security not to intertwine two threads of the same network, and that was what he was about to do. Not that he wanted to, but Yakovlev had insisted. And when the KGB *rezident* insisted, Gold listened.

Just before he had left New York to meet Fuchs in Santa Fe, Gold had been given an additional assignment by Yakovlev: he was to make a side trip to Albuquerque to pick up information from Corporal David Greenglass, an army technician employed at Los Alamos. Gold had never met Greenglass, and for identification Yakovlev had given him the back of a Jell-O box, cut in half. Greenglass would have the other half. Gold had objected strenuously. It was against all security for a cut-out to make two pickups on one mission. It endangered the mission, it endangered both agents, it endangered the cut-out. . . . Gold's arguments had been cut short when the *rezident* had said simply, "This is an order."

And so as the bus rolled through the outskirts of Albuquerque, Harry Gold was unhappy. For the first time in his espionage career he was breaking security, and it was all the more amazing that he was doing so at Yakovlev's insistence. Yakovlev, of all people, the most security-minded of them all—it proved once more that even the finest and most professional of spies are only flesh-and-blood human beings capable of carelessness and error. Gold knew how important the information was, both from Fuchs and from Greenglass. He knew how anxious Yakovlev was to get his report off to Center. He also knew that another cut-out had originally been assigned to the Greenglass pickup but had fallen ill. He knew all these things and he could understand the *rezident's* concern, but still, two pickups on one mission— it was all wrong. Resigned, Gold took his bag down from the overhead rack as the bus rolled to a stop. Orders are orders, more so in the KGB than in any other organization in the world. Gold climbed down from the bus and went to look for David Greenglass.

The young corporal and his even younger wife lived at the top of a steep flight of stairs at 209 North High Street. Gold was breathless when he reached the top of the stairs. He could barely gasp out the identifying phrase. "Julius sent me," he finally managed to say to the man in bathrobe and slippers who had opened the door. David Greenglass nodded and let him in. While the cut-out waited just inside the door, Greenglass shuffled over to a table, opened his wife's purse, and took out his half of the Jell-O box. Gold produced his half; they matched. Greenglass smiled for the first time, and relaxed.

"How is Julius?" he asked.

Gold shook his head impatiently. "Do you have any information for me?" he demanded.

Greenglass had information, plenty of it, but it had to be written up. In the meantime he wanted to talk about his sister, Ethel Rosenberg, and her husband Julius. Gold saw no reason to explain that he did not even know Julius or Ethel Rosenberg, that the name Julius was just part of a password to him. He did not want to talk about anything; he did not want the cup of coffee Ruth Greenglass insisted he should have, or the cookies she pressed on him. He just wanted out—out, out, out, of a bad security situation. He instructed Greenglass to write up the information, saying that he would be back at 3 P.M. Then he left.

When he returned that afternoon the report was ready. As if to solemnize the event, Greenglass was wearing his army uniform and Ruth had set out the inevitable coffee and cookies. Gold brushed aside the refreshments and studied the report. David Greenglass was a machinist who worked in one of the three top-secret machine shops at Los Alamos. His report consisted of several sheets of ruled white paper on which were schematic drawings of the flat-lens molds for detonating an atom bomb. Several other pages explained the letters and symbols in the sketches. Gold studied the report without comment; in truth, there was nothing he could say, for the sketches were meaningless to him. He nodded, put the report into an envelope in his pocket, then laid another envelope containing $500 on the table. Then he stood up and said that he had to go.

"So soon?" Ruth asked. He had not touched his coffee.

"I've got to go," Gold repeated. This, too, was basic security. Gold had trained himself to leave as soon as he received any documents. Before the transfer only one party was vulnerable; after the transfer they both were. To his irritation, the young couple insisted on accompanying him part of the way. He let them stay with him as far as the USO building down the street, then hinted broadly that he would prefer to go the rest of the way alone. David and Ruth finally understood. They turned into the USO building, and Gold walked on alone. When the young couple came out, he was gone.

Harry Gold reached New York on the evening of

June 5. That night he kept a prearranged rendezvous with Yakovlev in a quiet, out-of-the-way section of Brooklyn. The encounter was brief: no more than a chat on the street while Gold passed over two envelopes, the first marked "Doctor," the second marked "other." Then they separated. They met again two weeks later, and Yakovlev told Gold that the envelopes had caused a sensation in Moscow. Using words which from the *rezident* meant very high praise, Yakovlev told his cut-out that the information was "particularly excellent and very valuable."

Even that was an understatement. In one trip Gold had picked up all the details of the atomic bomb and its detonating device. Not the bomb that was tested the next month at Alamagordo, not the bomb that was to drop on Hiroshima, but the most advanced of the three types of atom bombs developed during the war: the implosion-type bomb that was to drop on Nagasaki and end World War II.

Harry Gold had been right to worry about making two pickups in one mission. It was a bad security slip. Anatoli Yakovlev was the most security-minded of *rezidents.* He always went by the book, insisting on tight security and unbreakable cover stories. It was because of this security-mindedness that none of his agents— members of the American KGB *rezidentura*—were ever mentioned in the GRU files that Gouzenko took from the Ottawa Embassy. Yakovlev was proud of that. After the Gouzenko disclosure had exposed the Canadian network, Colonel Zabotin had been recalled to Moscow where he had spent four years in jail. But the American ring had continued untouched, and all because of tight security. Then, in his anxiety to get two important reports off to Moscow, Yakovlev breached security for the first time in his career by insisting that Gold make both pickups. He didn't get away with it. The slip was to cost the *rezident* his network, and cost two of his agents their lives.

It started with Fuchs. After a year or so in prison, the doubts and fears which had caused the physicist to confess had grown to the point where he now felt compelled to aid his captors in any way possible. This was soul-cleaning on a grand scale, and for months Fuchs looked through thousands of pictures supplied by MI5 and the FBI in an attempt to pick out his American contact, whom he knew only as "Raymond." Working through MI5, Fuchs gave the FBI what he knew about Raymond, and it was little enough: a rough physical description, and the parenthetical note that Raymond had seemed to know something about chemistry. A thin enough lead to work on, but the FBI reasoned that Raymond must be from the East Coast since his first contact with Fuchs had been in New York. The Bureau eventually was able to concentrate its search on chemists who had either worked or lived in New York, Philadelphia, or Buffalo. Fifteen hundred photos of possible suspects were collected: chemists from the East Coast who matched the general description of Raymond. Sitting in his cell, Fuchs examined each picture carefully.

The first time around he identified no one. The second time around, he pointed to a picture of Harry Gold, and said, "I can't swear, but I'm pretty sure this is the man."

Gold was interviewed by FBI agents in the living room of his Philadelphia home. Outwardly, he was the picture of candor, eager to cooperate with the federal men. When he was shown a picture of Klaus Fuchs and asked to identify it, he smiled slightly and nodded. Of course he recognized the man, he had seen the same picture in the newspapers. "This is that English spy," he said, but he denied ever meeting Fuchs. When he was asked if he had ever been in Santa Fe, he smiled again and said that he had never been west of the Mississippi River.

To prove his desire to cooperate with the FBI, Gold agreed to pose for photographs, and to allow the agents to search his house. This time he was being too candid, and it was unnecessary: the agents had no warrant with them. The search began in Gold's bedroom, and ended fifteen minutes later when one of the agents looked behind a bookcase and found a map of Santa Fe. Clearly marked on it was the Castillo Bridge where Gold had rendezvoused with Fuchs.

It was an odd possession for a man who had never been west of the Mississippi, but it was not, in itself, incriminating. Gold could have given the agents any one of a dozen stories to explain the presence of the map. The story might have been believable or not, but the agents would have had to accept it. The map, by itself, was not evidence of even the flimsiest sort. Gold knew that, but instead of giving any one of the several stories that came quickly to his mind, he suddenly collapsed. Harry Gold, who had prided himself on being something close to a professional spy, sat down abruptly, and said, with an air of total defeat: "Well, it's time to say something. I'm the man to whom Fuchs gave his information."

Gold's collapse was not surprising, for he was not a professional but only a talented amateur. In espionage the difference between the two is more than a question of rank, or training, or even of ability. It is a question of dedication. The professional spy is working for the interests of his own country, and he has every right to be proud of the work he does. The amateur, however, is almost by definition a traitor. No matter how much his ideology supports his actions, the amateur spy lives with the knowledge that he is betraying his country, his family, his friends, the ingrained ideals of his childhood. It is an awful burden to carry, even for the most sophisticated, and when the pressure is applied the burden nearly always proves to be too heavy to bear. There are exceptions. Julius and Ethel Rosenberg were amateurs, but they never cracked; Reino Hayhanen was a Moscow-trained professional, but he cracked badly. But these exceptions aside, it is axiomatic that once an amateur spy is caught he reveals everything. Klaus Fuchs did, and now Harry Gold was about to.

Harry Gold made a general confession of all his espionage activities for the Yakovlev ring. He was arrested on a charge of espionage, pleaded guilty, and was sentenced to thirty years in prison. In his confession, Gold named David Greenglass as the army technician who had given him the plans for the flat-lens molds. Gold should never have seen Greenglass, should never even have heard his name, but because of Yakovlev's security slip two separate threads of the network had been joined. Now, instead of losing only one section of his *rezidentura*, Yakovlev was to lose it all.

Fuchs had confessed, Gold had confessed, and now it was the turn of David Greenglass to bare his soul. But the former army technician was a better business-man than either the physicist or the courier. Greenglass made a bargain with the FBI. He agreed to give them a detailed account of his espionage activities in which he accused his sister, Ethel Rosenberg, and her husband Julius of mesmerizing him into spying for the Russians. In return for this, the FBI agreed not to prosecute Ruth Greenglass, who had also been involved in the spy ring. Greenglass tried to get full immunity for himself, too, but the best deal he could get was the promise of a relatively light sentence.

This "light" sentence turned out to be fifteen years, but considering the sentence passed on the Rosenbergs, it was light indeed.

Like others of the new breed of spy, Julius and Ethel Rosenberg turned to Communism in the bitterness of the economic Depression of the nineteen thirties. During the early days of World War II they became part of Yakovlev's network, but without any specific duties.

Neither of the Rosenbergs was in a position to supply information to the Russians; their value lay in being *korrektirovchiki*, or recruiters, of likely informants. The most likely, by coincidence, turned out to be Ethel's younger brother, David.

It was not difficult to recruit young David Greenglass into the *apparat*, or network. He had always been emotionally dependent on his older sister, and he worshiped her husband Julius. David was only a twelve-year-old boy when Julius Rosenberg entered his life; by the time he was fourteen he was a member of the Young Communist League. Instead of diminishing as he grew older, this hero-worshiping attitude grew stronger, and when Julius suggested that he give information to the Russians, appealing to him on ideological as well as personal grounds, David agreed almost at once. He was in New York on furlough from Los Alamos when the suggestion was made. Two months later he was home on furlough again, this time with a batch of information about the Los Alamos project. Julius was delighted, and began to make plans for a little network of his own. For economic reasons, Ruth Greenglass had been living in New York while her husband was in the Army. Julius now suggested that she move to Albuquerque to be near David. That way, Julius explained, she could act as a courier between David and any cut-out sent down from New York. Ruth Greenglass wanted to know who was going to pay for all this, but Julius reassured her.

"All your expenses will be paid," he said. "The Russians will take care of the money."

Then with a deft piece of melodramatic stage business that entranced his young brother-in-law, Julius went into the kitchen and came out with a box of Jell-O. He stripped the back from the box and cut it raggedly in half. He put one half in his pocket and handed the other to the mystified David. It was an identification sign, he explained.

"If anyone comes to see you from me, he'll have the other half."

Of course, Julius Rosenberg was too disciplined a Communist to attempt running the Greenglass operation on his own. He reported back to Yakovlev, and at the same time turned over his half of the Jell-O box. It was shortly after this happened that the *rezident* made the fatal mistake of using one cut-out for two pickups.

The Yakovlev *rezidentura* was completely smashed by the disclosures made in the Greenglass confession. In addition to the Rosenbergs, several minor members of the ring were arrested, including Morton Sobell. Two other members, Morris and Lona Cohen, fled the country before the FBI learned of their connection with the ring. They escaped just in time to play more important roles seven years later in another major espionage case. Yakovlev, too, was named as a defendant in the same indictment brought against the Rosenbergs, but it was only a formality. The Russian had fled in plenty of time, back to Moscow and an unknown fate.

The trial, conviction, and execution of Julius and Ethel Rosenberg was less a matter of law than an emotional catharsis that left an indelible mark on the nation.

Despite the testimony of David Greenglass, the Rosenbergs insisted throughout their trial that they were innocent. After they were convicted they were offered all sorts of inducements, including their very lives, to confess and inform. In the face of this they never wavered from their original position, which was that they were innocent, persecuted victims of a capitalistic society. That they were guilty was never seriously doubted by any but the most gullible. But the staunchness of their attitudes, and their dignity in the shadow of the electric chair, won them the support of many people on a purely emotional basis. In addition, they were the first native Americans ever to receive the death penalty for espionage, a decision which many Americans felt to be excessive, if not actually vindictive.

This generation of sympathy for the Rosenbergs on emotional rather than logical grounds was accentuated by a worldwide campaign by the Communist press for their release. The Rosenberg case became one of the *causes célèbres* of the century, and for years it was impossible to discuss the case dispassionately. The case was in and out of the courts regularly, climbing the American judicial ladder of appeal after appeal. Two American presidents, Truman and Eisenhower, had the opportunity to commute the sentences; both refused. And while all this was going on the Rosenbergs sat in the death house in Sing Sing issuing statements and manifestos, propagandizing their cause right up to the minute when they were led, separately, into the execution chamber. In the face of overwhelming evidence they continued to insist that they were innocent. Julius and Ethel Rosenberg reached the high points of their lives in the death house at Sing Sing, playing the roles of Communist martyrs while half the world churned and agitated for their release. This international recognition seemed to give them an illusion of self-respect which they could have got in no other way. They could have saved themselves, but their lives had become secondary. Until the very moment of execution a telephone line was kept open between Sing Sing and the White House in case either of them decided to talk. But, supported by worldwide opinion, the Rosenbergs saw themselves slated for a niche in the Communist hagiography, and they preferred to die silently, rather than lose that chance of dubious immortality.

4 EDUCATION OF A SPY

Secret intelligence agents—even the best of them such as Rudolf Abel—may occasionally be born, but they are also made. In fact, the manual of the training section of the Soviet Secret Service for the year 1960 states candidly that, "any person can be taught to be a really outstanding master spy, provided he or she is *right* for this highly skilled profession. . . ." At first glance there appears to be a contradiction in this statement. How can *any* person be taught, if he has to be *right* for the profession in the first place?

The answer lies in an understanding of Communist jargon, for in this case *right* means ideologically right.

Only the most faithful, the members of the Communist Party or the Komsomol youth group, are considered as potential agents, and even they are screened so carefully and for such a long period of time that the candidate himself is often unaware that he is under consideration. This long-range recruitment program is basic to both the KGB and the GRU, and ensures that both agencies will get only the most suitable candidates and that no time will be wasted in training unlikely recruits.

The first step in the training of a Soviet intelligence agent, whether he be slated for the KGB or the GRU, is a four-month course at the Marx-Engels School at Gorky, near Moscow. The school is built well back from the street and is surrounded by high brick walls. All entrances are guarded by armed KGB officers, and each candidate as he enters must surrender his Party membership card, passport, and all other documents. For the duration of the course the candidate is a boarder at the school and is not allowed to leave the grounds for any reason short of discharge from the service.

Any eager young candidate who enters the Marx-Engels School with visions of espionage adventures is bound to be disappointed. Far from learning anything to do with the practical side of the spy trade, the students at the school spend the entire four months attending classes in which nothing is taught but *The History of the World Workers' Movement* and *The History of the Communist Party of the USSR*. Since these are two courses which every Party member has already studied and passed, the result is four months of boring routine. Nevertheless, each student must complete the course and pass the examinations before being sent on to the Lenin Technical School at Verkhovnoye.

This school is situated some ninety miles from the city of Kazan, in a desolate spot near the border of the Autonomous Tatar Soviet Republic. The huge complex of buildings stretches over several square miles. It can be approached only by a private road, and is completely inaccessible to anyone not connected with it. It is here that the practical side is espionage is taught.

The course at the Lenin Technical School lasts for one year, beginning with a month of intensive physical training. After this comes instruction in self-defense and the handling of firearms. Each of these classes lasts only one week, since most Communist Party members maintain a high standard of proficiency through weekly practice sessions. In addition, many of the candidates, those slated for the GRU, are army officers already at the expert level. With these basic matters out of the way, the recruit is ready for more advanced training. This takes the form of four courses essential to the education of the future agent.

Course number one is in the use of explosives, and takes place on the training ground in the northern part of the school. There the student learns the uses of dynamite, TNT, plastics, and other explosives. He also learns to make homemade bombs from whatever scraps of material may come to hand. Mock bridges and buildings are erected on the training grounds, and the students are taught to pick the most effective points for the placing of explosives, to plant the charges securely, and to detonate them from a safe distance. Also included in this training cycle is a course on the blowing of locks, strong-room doors, and safes. The last part of the course consists of detailed tuition on the fitting of small but highly effective explosives into cigarette boxes, lighters, pens, and other ordinary-looking articles.

The bugging course comes next. In this the student is trained in the tapping of telephone lines, the placing of high-powered microphones, and in the operation of tape and wire recorders. The KGB relies to a great extent on gimmicky devices, and the prospective agent is trained extensively in the use of microphones which are concealed within wristwatches and buttons, and connected to tiny wire recorders carried in the pocket.

The third course deals with the operation of portable radio receiver-transmitters, including the use of special appliances for broadcasting at high speed. These devices enable the agent to cut the time of transmission to mere seconds, and thus escape the attention of counterespionage monitoring stations. The student is trained to service his radio, to dismantle and reassemble it under field conditions, and to repair the set using improvised material. Students also receive intensive training in coding and decoding methods, and it would be worthwhile at this point to take a detailed look at the code systems used by the KGB.

Cryptology, the science of secret communications, embodies both codes and ciphers. Basically, codes use symbols or groups of letters to mean whole words or phrases. Ciphers use single letters or numbers or symbols as substitutes for other single letters or numbers. Soviet agents communicate with Center both in code and in cipher, since a simple cipher, in which one letter is substituted for another, can be easily broken. This is because in any language, letters reappear according to well-established principles of frequency. In English, for example, the letter "e" appears more often than any other. Therefore, modern spying requires a more complex system.

The KGB and the GRU, and indeed all major intelligence organizations, use a sophisticated system of miniature cipher pads known as gammas. These pads, which are no bigger than a postage stamp, are made of nitrated cellulose which will burn in an instant. Each pad contains up to 250 pages, and on each page dozens of five-digit number groups are printed. The pages are alternatively red and black, the agent in the field using the black pages to encipher outgoing messages, and the red pages to decipher incoming messages. Each page on the pad is used only one time, and then destroyed. This makes the cipher unbreakable, since the only other copy of the pad is in Moscow Center. Since the number groups are selected at random and vary from page to page, they are meaningless to anyone trying to crack the cipher.

Gamma cipher pads are used in conjunction with a table of numbers known as the Monome-Dinome chart. This complicated-sounding procedure is actually nothing more than a very simple way of encoding (as opposed to enciphering) messages. To make such a chart, the espionage agent first memorizes a key word or phrase, which is then used as the basis of the table. Number values assigned to the letters in the key word are then used as the basis for a code for the entire alphabet. (The key word in Hayhanen's code was *snegopa*, the Russian word for snowfall.) Here is a simple example in English, from a typical Russian code. The key word is PLAYER, and the other letters follow in alphabetical order in groups of six. The number values are assigned *vertically* on the table, and the numbers used, in this case, are 00–09, 21–29, and 40–48.

00	05	21	26	41	45
P	L	A	Y	E	R
01	06	22	27	42	46
B	C	D	F	G	H
02	07	23	28	43	47
I	J	K	M	N	O
03	08	24	29	44	48
Q	S	T	U	V	W
04	09	25	40		
X	Z	&	•		

In this particular table there are twenty-eight number groups, one for each letter, and one each for a period and for the symbol "&" which is used as a signal that the message is about to change from letters to numbers.

Using such a chart, the agent next encodes the message to be sent, working in eight-digit groups. Suppose that the first word—*meet*—resulted in the number 2841-4124. The agent then turns to his gamma pad. The first number in his message is the page number of the pad which tells Center which sheet he is using. He then begins the actual message. Suppose the first gamma number is 68751539. To this he adds his first eight-digit group of 28414124. The result, 86165653, is the first group of the message which is sent to Center. This is because in adding figures, the KGB uses modular arithmetic, which means that numbers are not carried over to the next column. Thus:

$$28414124$$
$$68751539$$
$$\overline{86165653}$$

To decipher the message, Center simply subtracts the gamma number, in this case 68751539, from the total and works backward. The cipher is unbreakable because each page of the gamma pad giving the code is used only once. It was because of this that the message in the hollow nickel lay unbroken in the files of the FBI for so long. Even the sophisticated electronic computers of the National Security Agency at Fort Meade, Maryland, were unable to crack it. Not until Hayhanen defected in 1957 was the FBI able to read the message.

The last stage of the twelve-month course at the Lenin Technical School is spent on practical photography. The

main training concentrates on the handling of microfilm cameras, and students must become fully qualified
to take perfect copies of documents, technical drawings,
and maps. Heavy emphasis is also placed on the reduc-
tion of messages into microdots which can then be concealed under postage stamps or false periods at the end
of typewritten sentences. Although Soviet agents working abroad are equipped with efficient microfilm cameras, they are also trained in the use of popular local
brands so as not to be handicapped if anything should
happen to their own.

The final examinations at the Lenin Technical School
take an entire week to complete. But passing the examinations is not, in itself, a pass into Soviet intelligence.
A long course of specialized training awaits the prospective agent, but for the moment he is allowed to relax.
After twelve months of this intensive training, the grad-
uating students are sent for a month's holiday to the
Oktyabr Recreation Home in the Caucasian mountains.
There, beside the waters of the Kyslovodsk spa, they
await the decisions of the KGB selection boards which
will determine their futures.

Although the rate of failure at the Lenin Technical
School is extremely low, not all those who pass become
secret agents for the Soviet Union. While the graduates
vacation at the Caucasian spa, their records are reviewed by the experienced officers of the KGB Selection Board. The successful candidates are divided into
two groups: those who are suitable for home duties, and

those who are suitable for foreign service. Members of the first group are assigned to KGB headquarters for careers in any of the varied departments of Russian internal security, such as counterespionage, border patrol, secret police, and others. It is from the members of the second group that the secret agents are drawn.

Members of this second group are first assigned to Moscow Center for what are called "assessment duties." This assignment can last up to one year, and during that time the cadet agent is expected to familiarize himself with the routine of every department in the organization. The novices study not only the routine duties of the divisional officers, but also read the daily comprehensive reports of agents in the field and acquaint themselves with the local conditions of the countries in which they may be called upon to operate. It is only after this period of on-the-job training that the cadet agent is sent on to the specialized schools to complete his education as a spy.

The training at the specialized schools is little more than a graduate course in the techniques that the agent learned at the Lenin Technical School, with one exception. This is the school for environmental rehabilitation, where the agent literally learns to forget that he is Russian. There are several of these schools, all operated along the same lines. The one which processes agents headed for the English-speaking world is known simply as Gaczyna.

Gaczyna covers over four hundred square miles in the area southeast of Kuibyshev. As might be expected, the entire zone is sealed off from the rest of the world and guarded by detachments of the KGB. The students are flown into the area in special KGB aircraft, and upon arrival find themselves in foreign surroundings. The school is divided into four distinct sections: the United States section in the northwest; the Canadian section in the north; the United Kingdom section in the northeast; the Australian, New Zealand, Indian, and South African sections in the south.

The length of time that a student stays at Gaczyna depends entirely upon the needs of Soviet intelligence. The minimum term is two years, and students have been known to stay as long as ten. For if he were not so before, the student who enters Gaczyna is totally the creature of the KGB, and he will stay at Gaczyna until such time as he is needed in the field. It is a basic tenet of KGB and GRU training that if a man assumes a new identity over a period of years, he never loses it, not even under torture, brainwashing, or injections of truth drugs. Whether or not this is so, results have shown that most graduates of Gaczyna, when captured in the field, have clung tenaciously to their own cover stories without breaking.

Total immersion in a new way of life begins the moment the student arrives at Gaczyna. He is taken at once to that section of the school which represents the country to which he has been assigned, and for as long as he stays at the school he will never leave that sector. Every division of Gaczyna is a true reproduction of buildings and streets, restaurants, snack bars, and other public establishments in countries of the English-speaking world. In the United States section, for example, there is a "city" area which seems to resemble a composite representation of downtown Detroit, Los Angeles, and Philadelphia—minus the skyscrapers, of course. The "town" area is a large section of some anonymous town of 10,000 population in the midwestern or western United States, the kind of town which might be located some five miles from a missile site or important aircraft factory. For specific assignments and at designated times of the year, the town is given a specific location, such as Alabama or Arizona, so that the trainees may familiarize themselves with local dialects, customs and geographical peculiarities.

Everyone in the area dresses in clothes particular to the country, and the students live in hotels and boarding houses which are identical to those in England or America. All employees in the area—waitresses, bus drivers, shop clerks—including the language instructors themselves, are former citizens of the country involved: foreign Communists who have become Soviet citizens and have qualified for these jobs. Once assigned to Gaczyna, without exception, they will stay there for the rest of their lives.

Thus, from the very first day the student is in the hands of genuine ex-citizens of the country of his "adoption," and it is from them that he learns the correct pronunciation, sentence structure, and intonation of the language he must learn to speak as a native.

In the American section the student drinks milk

shakes and eats hamburgers at a typical drugstore. He drives a Ford or a Chevrolet to school every day, and if he exceeds the speed limit he is given a ticket and bawled out by an American-type traffic cop. He listens to American music, sees only American films, and pays for all his purchases in dollars. During the summertime he even watches videotaped television broadcasts of recent major league baseball games in order to familiarize himself with the national game. He learns that Americans generally pay more attention to their clothes than do Russians, and so he makes sure to have a clean suit and well-polished shoes at all times. He learns to change his shirt and socks daily, to wear sunglasses and short-sleeved shirts in the summer, to read the sports page of his newspaper first, and to stand with his hands in his pockets and chew gum in a natural manner. In every possible way he learns to live like an American, to think like an American, to *be* an American.

All of this is in addition to daily instruction in the English language. The one unbreakable rule at Gaczyna is that Russian must never, under any circumstances, be spoken. To utter even one word in Russian is grounds for dismissal from the school, and the rule is obeyed religiously. The result of this rigid training is a totally new personality. There have even been instances where an agent has forgotten how to speak his native tongue. One such case came to light through Oleg Penkovskiy, the GRU officer who secretly supplied British intelligence with information before he was caught by the Russians and shot. In his memoirs, Penkovskiy mentioned his friend, Shcherbakov, who had spent seven years at

Gaczyna, and then an additional eight years as an illegal agent in the field. During those fifteen years Shcherbakov became so completely Americanized that he forgot how to speak Russian and needed the help of a translator in order to give his verbal reports when he returned to Moscow Center.

Before an agent is sent into the field he must undergo one further test of his ability and integrity. He is arrested by the KGB and subjected to the most ingenious methods of interrogation in order to see how well he will stand up to similar methods employed by opposing counterespionage services. The procedure is carried out in a standard pattern and it never varies.

The candidate is arrested individually, and does not know if anyone shares his fate. He is given no reason for his arrest, and is taken to the dreaded Lubianka Prison. There he is marched off to the Investigation Block and ordered to stand motionless facing a wall with his hands clasped behird his head. As one agent who endured this treatment reported: "You begin to feel every part of the body, each joint of a finger—it is as though tons of weariness rush down into your every joint. Suddenly you break out in a cold sweat. Your whole body begins to itch unbearably. You feel compelled to scratch yourself, but the guard notices the movement and threatens to blow your brains out. You think it impossible to endure any longer, but you do endure it. And hours and hours drag slowly, painfully by."

Eventually the agent is taken to the office of the interrogator in charge and accused of being a foreign spy who has managed to worm his way into Soviet intelligence. The agent, stunned and unable to grasp how this could happen to him, denies everything. When he tries to explain, he is shouted down. When he refuses to confess, he is threatened with immediate execution. He is subjected to all the standard forms of brainwashing: little sleep, constant interrogation, bright lights in his eyes, and even some physical violence. The cycle goes on for days, until the interrogator in charge is satisfied that the agent is "break-proof." Then, the mock arrest over, the agent is taken to another room where he is addressed by a high official of the KGB. Everything is explained and, strange as it may seem, none of the agents seem to mind having been subjected to such treatment. They all appear happy that the nightmare has been only another test, and they all agree that the precaution is in their own interests. Proud of their ability to resist professional interrogation, they are now ready for the field.

*The Dynamos,
the KGB soccer team,
in London in 1945*
(RADIO TIMES HULTON)

*The Lubianka building near the Kremlin,
headquarters of the KGB* (UPI)

Richard Sorge,
Soviet agent in
Japan during
World War II
(WIDE WORLD)

"Master spy"
Rudolf Abel,
Soviet agent in
the U.S. in the
1950's (UPI)

Alan Nunn May, British physicist who gave
atomic secrets to Russia in the 1940's (UPI)

Russian defector Igor Gouzenko, masked to conceal his identity,
is interviewed by a reporter in 1945 (WIDE WORLD)

Atom spy Klaus
Fuchs in 1959,
after his release
from prison (UPI)

William Skardon
(left) and Henry
Arnold, British
MI5 agents,
at Fuchs' trial
in 1950 (UPI)

Ethel and Julius Rosenberg, sentenced to death in 1953 for espionage
(BROWN BROTHERS)

Harry Gold in 1966, after serving 16 years of his sentence for espionage
(WIDE WORLD)

*British spy
Kim Philby,
who fled to Russia
in 1963* (UPI)

*Greville Wynne,
a British agent,
on trial in Moscow
for espionage* (UPI)

Oleg Penkovskiy, accused with Wynne of espionage, was found guilty by a Soviet military court and executed in May 1963 (UPI)

Materials used as evidence at Penkovskiy's trial: miniature cameras and film, coded notebooks, and a portable transistor radio set (WIDE WORLD)

Gordon Lonsdale, former head of a spy ring that stole British naval secrets for the Russians, was exchanged for Greville Wynne in 1964 (WIDE WORLD)

Allen Dulles (left) and Admiral William Raborn (right) with Richard M. Helms, present director of the CIA (WIDE WORLD)

An East Berlin policeman points to the secret tunnel through which CIA agents tapped Soviet telephone lines (WIDE WORLD)

A U-2 jet plane, designed to collect information from fifteen miles above the earth (UPI)

Francis Gary Powers, whose U-2 plane was shot down in May 1960, on trial in Moscow for spying (UPI)

The crew of the U.S.S. Pueblo, freed after eleven months of captivity in North Korea (WIDE WORLD)

5 THE OLD SCHOOL TIE

Every working day in Moscow a stocky, middle-aged Englishman with clear, blue eyes arrives at KGB headquarters at Number 2 Dzershinsky Square, there to perform his duties as the chief adviser to that section of the KGB which operates against Great Britain and the United States. He is a man quite remarkably equipped for the job—for as the most successful double agent of modern times, this man, Kim Philby, would very likely now be head of the British Secret Service had he not been uncovered and forced to flee to Russia in 1963. At the time of his defection it seemed impossible to his many well-placed friends that Harold Adrian Russel

Philby, O.B.E., one-time darling of the British Establishment, should ever have turned traitor; but in fact the turning had occurred years before. Philby became a Communist during his university days and, by his own later admission, became a serving officer in the KGB in 1934, shortly after he came down from Cambridge.

Philby's name has been permanently linked in the history of espionage with those of Guy Burgess and Donald Maclean. All three were Cambridge men, British civil servants, and, ultimately, Russian spies. It is impossible to tell the story of one without those of the others. Together the three men formed the microcosm of a Soviet spy network that operated for years within the British Foreign Office and the Secret Service. Probably no other KGB network was ever so successful.

In the jargon of Soviet intelligence, Philby was the *novator*, Maclean was the *istochnik*, and Burgess was the *korretirovchik*. These terms, which go back to the days of the Czarist Cheka, describe the three main functions of the espionage network. The *novator*, who is similar to a *rezident*, is the planner in charge of operations in a target country. He works in close collaboration with the *korretirovchik*, the spotter who recruits the *istochnik*, or actual source of information.

They met at Cambridge. Kim Philby, nicknamed after the character in Kipling's novel, had been born in India, the son of Harry St. John Philby, who was a friend of Lawrence of Arabia and himself a famed Arabist. The tall, thin, austere Maclean was the son of a Liberal cabinet minister. By contrast, Guy Burgess was a heavy, slovenly young man whose appearance belied a brilliant wit and intelligence. All three were Communists at college, a not uncommon occurrence in the early nineteen thirties, but they were bound together by more than ideological ties. All three were products of that undefinable ruling body which the British call simply the Establishment. As members of the Establishment, Philby, Burgess, and Maclean were bound by birth, class, wealth, speech, and education, not only to each other but to the select group of men who have always governed England. This bond, so peculiarly English, was to serve the trio well in future years.

When the three came down from Cambridge their careers diverged. Maclean entered the Foreign Office in 1935, spent the war years in London, and in 1944 was sent to Washington as first secretary at the British Embassy there. Burgess, meanwhile, did some newspaper work, some broadcasting for the BBC, and during the war seemed to slip rather casually into the British counterintelligence corps, a natural move for an educated Englishman. A year later he returned officially to the BBC, but actually he remained in intelligence work attached to the Special Operations, Executive. In 1944 he, too, joined the Foreign Office.

As to Philby's career, the world knows little more than the surface details. We know that he was a journalist during the Spanish Civil War, covering the winning Franco side for *The Times* of London. We know that during World War II he served in British counterintelligence, and that after the war he remained an intelligence agent operating under Foreign Office cover. We know that he was posted to Istanbul in 1947, and that two years later he was sent to Washington. All this time, of course, he had been working secretly for the KGB. The amount of information he was able to pass along to Center during this period must have been more than satisfactory to his superiors in Moscow, but the best was yet to come.

Philby was posted to Washington with the covering rank of first secretary in the Diplomatic Service, but his actual job was to act as liaison with the director of the newly formed American Central Intelligence Agency.

It is impossible to calculate the amount of damage that Philby did in this sensitive position: his success cannot be measured solely in coups and countercoups, although there were enough of these. Perhaps the best example is the little-known but frightening tale of the Albanian debacle.

The tiny country on the Adriatic went Communist in the aftermath of World War II, and many of the non-Communist Resistance leaders who cooperated with the British and Americans during the war were imprisoned and eventually executed. A few of the more prominent patriots, however, managed to escape to Italy and Greece, and under their leadership an Albanian Freedom Movement was formed. The organization was financed by both the CIA and the British Secret Service, whose concern was not only the retaking of Albania, but also its eventual use as a base for American rocket installations strategically pointed northward toward the

Soviet satellite bloc. The Italian and Greek governments, neither of which was happy at the thought of such a close Communist neighbor, were brought into the plans, and both were pleased to provide training grounds for the Albanian volunteers.

Philby had been in Washington about one year when the Albanian project started to move, and he soon took it for his own. This was not difficult for him to do, for he was much admired by his American friends at the CIA, not only for his great personal charm but also for his seemingly uncanny grasp of Soviet operating procedure. He seemed to know just what was going to happen when, and his American counterparts were more than content to have him as the political and strategic chief of the Albanian enterprise. He made several flying visits to the Albanian Freedom Movement training centers in Italy and Greece, all the while passing on detailed reports of what he saw to the local Soviet agents. Moscow Center conveyed the information to the KGB station in Albania, which in turn notified the Albanian Communist authorities. With no waste of time, Russian and Bulgarian troops were flown secretly into Albania to await the invasion.

Several months later the first units of the Albanian Freedom Army crossed the Greek frontier in a venture that was doomed before it began. The invading army was equipped with nothing heavier than machine guns and mortars, and they were soon surrounded by a Communist army boasting Russian field guns, heavy tanks, and spotter aircraft. It was a desperate, hopeless struggle, and within six weeks the adventure had ended in disaster. Less than two hundred of the volunteers survived to struggle back across the Greek frontier; the rest were killed in battle or shot by firing squads after being captured. In addition, the villagers who had given food and shelter to the invaders suffered horribly. Several villages were burned to the ground, people were shot without trial, and more than two thousand others were imprisoned. Two months after the invasion began, the Albanian government could boast that it had been repulsed by "the heroic Army and Militia of the People's Republic."

Kim Philby had accomplished a major coup at no risk to himself. There was no inquest over the Albanian affair in either Washington or London. The few American officials who had known of the enterprise regretfully wrote it off as "bad luck." Philby was called home to London to report, but only because the Foreign Office and the Secret Service preferred not to put such reports in writing. Once on home grounds, Philby simply blamed the "clumsy Americans" for the debacle and his explanation was accepted without question. He was returned to Washington to continue his good work.

The good work he did there, however—the good work for his Soviet masters—was not confined to adventures such as the Albanian coup. No one can estimate the amount of information that passed through Philby's hands and on to Moscow Center, but the ultimate blow that he struck for the KGB came *after* his defection, not before. For when the knowledge became public that the British Secret Service's liaison man to the CIA had been a Russian agent, the close-knit Anglo-American intelligence relationship was so damaged that it has never been the same since.

Just as there is no way of estimating the amount of information that Philby passed to the KGB, there is also no way of knowing how long he might have continued to do so, had it not been for the actions of the two weaker members of the original trinity, Burgess and Maclean. But for them Philby might have gone all the way to the top; in 1950 it was inside information that he was to be the next head of British intelligence. By English standards he had every attribute for the position: birth, education, social standing, high intelligence, a successful career, and the all-important ability to get along with the "clumsy Americans." But the two weak links snapped and the chain was broken.

Both Burgess and Maclean had long been noted for their scandalous behavior. Maclean, a married man, was a confirmed alcoholic; Burgess, a bachelor, was an overt homosexual. Despite this, because of the unwritten code which decrees that the Establishment must take care of its own, they both had risen high in the Foreign Office. By 1950, Burgess had joined Philby in Washington with the position of second secretary to the British Embassy, and Maclean had been appointed head of the American Department in London. It was during this period that their espionage careers flourished, but the end was in sight. For several years the British counterintelligence organization, the MI5, had known of a security leak in the Foreign Office. By 1951 they had narrowed down the suspects to one: Donald Maclean. In any other country this would have meant an immediate suspension from the Foreign Office and a thorough investigation, but not in England. Maclean's associates could not believe that an English gentleman could be guilty of such behavior. MI5 moved slowly on the case, so slowly that Philby, in his sensitive position, was able to learn of their suspicions and warn Maclean through Burgess.

At this time Burgess had troubles of his own. Because of his personally indiscreet behavior in Washington he had finally been ordered home to London where he was asked to resign from the Foreign Office. He alerted Maclean to his danger, and on May 25 the two of them drove to Southampton and boarded the S.S. *Falaise* for Saint-Malo in France. They were not to be seen again publicly until February 1956 when they surfaced in Moscow. There they stated blandly that they had come to the Soviet Union to work for better understanding between East and West. They also supplied the gratuitous information to reporters that "at Cambridge we both had been Communists . . . we neither of us have ever been Communist agents."

The last statement was necessary for the protection of Philby, who had been quietly summoned home after the disappearance of Burgess and Maclean. Because of his close connection with the two fugitives, he was asked to resign from British intelligence. He was not accused of any crime, never charged or brought to trial. In the tradition of the Establishment, he was simply asked to resign; and as an English gentleman, he complied with the request. Although questions were asked in the House of Commons, the Establishment once again took care of its own. Harold Macmillan, then the Foreign Secretary, assured the House that no evidence had been found to show that Philby was responsible for warning either Burgess or Maclean, and he added, "I have no reason to conclude that Mr. Philby has at any time betrayed the interests of this country. . . ." The old school tie was still flapping bravely in Britain's political breezes.

That should have been the end of it. Burgess and Maclean were irrevocably lost, Philby was fired and discredited, and the Establishment had covered the whole sad affair with a coat of first-class whitewash. That should have been the end of it but, incredibly, there was more to come. Some time in 1956 the Foreign Office went to *The Observer*, one of England's Sunday newspapers, on behalf of Kim Philby. Philby was down and out, said the people at the Foreign Office, and he needed a job. They assured David Astor of *The Observer* that the one-time intelligence official had completely severed his connections with the British Secret Service, and they asked, as a humane gesture, that he be given a job. Once again, the orderly world of English gentlemen took over. *The Observer* hired Philby and, splitting the cost with another newspaper, *The Economist*, sent him to Beirut in Lebanon, as their Middle East correspondent.

That Philby did some sort of British intelligence work there has never been proven—that is to say, the British have never admitted it—but unquestionably he continued to supply to Moscow whatever information came his way. For almost seven years after he had been officially discredited he again operated as a double agent, although on a lower level than before. He had many friends in Beirut from better days, including several highly placed CIA agents, and he was able to move once again in the world of international espionage with the unofficial blessing of the Foreign Office. And, as in his Washington post, he might still be there today but for a sensational but unpublicized change in the leadership of the British Secret Service.

Sir Dick White, the head of MI5, Britain's counterintelligence corps, had never been one of those who joined in the chorus to exonerate Philby after the Burgess and Maclean affair. In fact, he had been the prime initiator in the move to have Philby fired. When he learned that the Foreign Office was secretly using Philby's services again, Sir Dick was appalled. He was convinced that if Philby were not tried for treason, he should at least be barred from any contact with the espionage community. He got his chance to do something about this in 1956 when an intramural battle between Britain's two intelligence arms—MI6 and MI5, intelligence and counterintelligence respectively—was settled with MI5 triumphant. Several years later, in the aftermath of the battle, White was offered the top post in MI6, and he moved into it much like a conquering general occupying enemy territory. He was now Philby's boss, and one of his first moves in his new post was to order a reinvestigation of the Burgess-Maclean-Philby affair. With that kind of handwriting on the wall, it was time for Philby to make his final move. On January 23, 1963, instead of attending a dinner party in Beirut, he slipped aboard a Russian freighter lying in the harbor. The ship sailed on the morning tide, starting Philby on the long journey to Moscow, where he lives today, functioning as a colonel in the KGB and staying clear of the limelight except, of course, for those occasions when his superiors find it useful to expose his exploits to the world.

In the uproar that followed Philby's disappearance, questions again were asked in the House of Commons. This time the Conservative government admitted that Philby had been the man who had warned Burgess and Maclean, but no one would say why he had been readmitted to intelligence work. George Brown, later the Foreign Secretary in the Wilson government, asked the most telling question: "The Foreign Office asked the man to resign for reasons that had to do with his past political associations. Why did the Foreign Office then take the initiative to get a newspaper to employ him in the Middle East? The Foreign Office is not normally an employment agency. Why did they do that?"

There was no reply, but everyone knew the answer: it had been the gentlemanly thing to do.

The British intelligence system which Kim Philby so ably compromised differs from the Russian in one important aspect: the British system is as diversified as the Russian is centralized. All functions of Soviet security and espionage lie under the watchful eye of the KGB, but British intelligence is composed of three separate and equal major organizations, plus drops and snippets of other bureaus which operate as they will.

The organization responsible for internal security and counterespionage at home is known as MI5, and is perhaps the most famous and romantic of Britain's intelligence services. It is roughly equivalent to the American FBI, but with certain major differences, for MI5 is not established in law. No statute covers its existence and it is not recognized by common law. In fact, its operations are so carefully cloaked in mystery that until 1963 very few people in Britain, including Members of Parliament, knew that MI5 was responsible not to the Prime Minister, but to the Home Secretary.

This unusual situation began in 1909 when MI5 was established by Captain Vernon Kell as the branch of military intelligence devoted to the capturing of enemy spies. The office was formed unofficially, was given the sanction of the government of that day, and has continued in this fashion through two World Wars and the Cold War to the present. It has long ceased to have any connection with the War Office and is known only to the public as MI5, or Military Intelligence. In official circles it is known as the Security Service, but the public name is difficult to shake.

The second major difference between MI5 and the FBI is that the members of the British organization are simply ordinary citizens in the eyes of the law and have no more power than any other British subject. They may not enter premises without the permission of the owner, and they have no special powers of search or seizure. Most important, they cannot make an arrest! In no other country does a counterespionage service have so little actual power, but MI5 compensates for this with a close working collaboration with the Special Branch of Scotland Yard. MI5 does all the preliminary work of investigation; when it is time to make an arrest the Special Branch steps in and does what is necessary.

Despite this apparently makeshift arrangement, MI5 has scored many successes in the period since World War II, among the most notable being the Portland Naval Secrets case, the exposure of spies such as Vassal, Blake, Burgess, Maclean, and, eventually, Kim Philby. The operations of the office are designed to preserve its anonymity. When MI5 is investigating a suspect it uses a specially trained field force for observation. When a spy is uncovered, an immediate arrest is avoided when possible. MI5 prefers to keep the agent under surveillance, rather than arrest him, for two reasons: continued observation will often uncover other members of the same network, and, equally important, total surveillance is often the best way of nullifying the enemy's work. Eventually an arrest must be made by the Special Branch, and when that happens the MI5 people melt into the background in order to preserve the anonymity of their officers and techniques. Prosecution is always by the police, and it is only on the rarest occasions that MI5 personnel appear in court to give evidence.

One of those occasions was in 1963 during Lord Radcliffe's Tribunal of Inquiry into the Vassal case. It was announced that the director-general of the Security Service (MI5) would give evidence anonymously, and spectators were warned that any person who recognized this man must keep the knowledge to himself. Writing of that inquiry, Rebecca West described the scene: "The tall doors opened, an impressive figure walked in, and sat down in the witness chair and answered a few questions. . . . Then he strode out, his anonymity undoubtedly making the spectacle more enjoyable. . . . But it was hard to avoid the suspicion that the enemies of our country probably have a fair idea who the head of the Security Service is, and probably his full name, the date of his birth, his life history, the color of his eyes, and his weight. . . . "

In another account of the proceedings, Chapman Pincher of the *Daily Express* wrote: "His identity is known to every foreign agent worth his keep. His name will be bandied about today in a score of London clubs."

In fact the director-general at this time was Sir Roger Hollis, whose passion for anonymity went so far that when he was knighted by the Queen his occupation was mentioned in the Honours List as being "lately attached to the Ministry of Defence." Sir Roger later became an unfortunate casualty of the Profumo affair, losing his job because of the controversial role that MI5 played in that case. His successor listed himself with equal care when knighted in 1967 as "Jones, Edward Martin Furnival, attached to War Office."

The positive side of British espionage is the province of the Secret Service, known to the public as MI6. If a comparison were to be made, MI6 is roughly equivalent to the Covert Plans division of the American CIA, and is the operational intelligence arm which sends spies into other countries. The office was first organized during World War I by Sir Mansfield Cumming of the Royal Navy. He was known to his associates simply by the initial "C," and although he has been dead for many years, the head of MI6, whatever his name may be, is still traditionally called "C." This is the position— changed to "M" for the purposes of fiction—which the late Ian Fleming made known to millions of readers in his James Bond stories. The head of MI6 from 1939 to 1951 was Major-General Sir Stewart Menzies, under whom Fleming served, and who was used by the author as the model for "M." The present-day "C" is Sir Dick Goldsmith White, one of the most powerful men in England, and one who has had the rare opportunity to serve as head of both MI5 and MI6.

As the Philby case showed too clearly, British intelligence traditionally draws upon the Oxford and Cambridge graduates of the Establishment for its recruits. This tradition goes back as far as the sixteenth century and Sir Francis Walsingham, Secretary of State to Queen Elizabeth and the founder of England's first national secret service. Walsingham hired the brightest students from Oxford and Cambridge and sent them abroad to infiltrate the courts of England's enemies. British intelligence today, despite the reforms that followed the Profumo and Philby affairs, is still something of a gentleman's sport, and British agents are expected to play the game. The big difference in the service between Walsingham's day and today is that MI6 operatives are still gentlemen, but they are certainly not amateurs. Recruits for both MI5 and MI6 receive highly specialized training at schools quite similar to those run by the KGB. The difference between the two systems is only in degree. England has no equivalent to Gaczyna where Russian agents train for up to ten years, but the course of training that the British agent gets in the arts of espionage is fully as comprehensive as that of his Russian counterpart.

As does the KGB, the MI6 uses the mock arrest as part of its training procedure. Once again, however, the difference is in the degree and the results are often comical. In one case it led to an uproarious mix-up in which an innocent and respectable London businessman was accused of kidnapping.

It all began when two MI6 recruits were sent on a training exercise designed to teach them the art of interrogation. Their subject was to be another MI6 recruit being trained in how to *resist* interrogation. The first two were given a description of the subject and told that he could be found every day tailing the Home Secretary, Sir David Maxwell Fyfe, as he went to his office. The assignment: capture the subject and interrogate him.

At the appointed hour Sir David, who knew nothing of the training exercise, left his home. The two trainees at once pounced on the man walking directly behind Sir David and bundled him into a waiting car. Despite his protests they took him to an apartment in Old Brompton Road which had been loaned to MI6 for the exercise and proceeded to interrogate him. Terrified, the kidnapped man protested his innocence as the two trainees searched his clothing for hidden messages, sat him under bright lights, and subjected him to standard interrogation technique. The grilling went on for several hours, but despite all their efforts the trainees were unable to break the man. And for a very good reason: he was simply a low-level government clerk who had been on his way to work when MI6 abducted him.

After hours of fruitless questioning the trainees finally realized that they had grabbed the wrong man. Keeping up a good front, they warned him to say nothing of what had happened, and then released him. The clerk, of course, went straight to the police with the story and led them back to Old Brompton Road. There, just to complicate the farce, he pointed out the wrong apartment, one belonging to a respectable businessman who indignantly denied any part in the kidnapping. As the police hauled him off for questioning, his wife, hysterical over what was happening, called the *Daily Express*, and within minutes reporters were swarming over the building. News of the fiasco reached a Foreign Office official who called the deputy director of MI6 and warned him that things were getting out of hand. MI6 in turn called MI5 and asked for help. MI5 called in the Chief Press Censor who finally persuaded the newspaper to kill the story on the ground that it would jeopardize American opinion of British security. As for the real subject, the trainee who was supposed to have been following Sir David Maxwell Fyfe, the censor explained: "It was really most unfortunate. He missed his train."

The third major British secret service oversees the intelligence activities of the Royal Army, Navy, and Air Force. Known variously as the Directorate of Service Intelligence and the Joint Intelligence Bureau, the organization is something less than secret. Unlike his more glamorous MI cousins, the chief of the agency, who has the title of Director-General of Intelligence, is a public figure and is openly listed as an officer of the Ministry of Defence. In addition to the service agencies, the Director-General of Intelligence has two non-military directorates under him: one for scientific intelligence, the other for economic intelligence.

These three men, the heads of MI6 and MI5 and the Director-General of Intelligence, are the three chiefs of British intelligence. All three report to the chairman of the Joint Intelligence Committee which is part of the Foreign Office, but the chiefs themselves are to a great degree independent of control. The Joint Intelligence Committee acts as a coordinator for the three agencies and can make its influence felt, but it has no final authority.

At various times in history, other British espionage organizations have been created to perform particular missions. The best known of these was the Special Operations, Executive, which was formed during World War II with a simple directive from Prime Minister Winston

Churchill: "And now set Europe ablaze." The mission of the SO,E, which was independent of MI6 and MI5, was to encourage resistance and sabotage in Nazi-occupied countries. Its operational chief was Sir Colin Gubbins, who, borrowing the MI6 fashion, was known by the initial "M." With headquarters in London's Baker Street, the SO,E operated under several pseudonyms, among them the Inter-Service Research Bureau and the Joint Technical Board. SO,E operatives parachuted regularly into Nazi-controlled territory, and the organization was responsible for a huge amount of destructive work done by the Resistance. Trains were derailed, factories exploded, and troop movements hampered, with the SO,E providing the arms, technical assistance, and the coordination to make the work possible. After the war the SO,E was disbanded and, much like its American counterpart, the OSS, its people were absorbed by the more conventional intelligence agencies.

Public knowledge of espionage activities is understandably sketchy, and what we do know generally comes to us in the form of failures. The results of successful operations are never disclosed; it is only when a spy is captured and a network exposed that we learn a bit more of the covert business of spying that goes on around us daily. Thus, any history of modern espionage tends to be a record of failures. Some of the failures, however, are magnificent ones, with the agent exposed only after a long and successful career. Such was the case of Rudolf Abel, such was the case of Kim Philby, and, to the credit of the British MI6, such was the case of Oleg Penkovskiy.

6 OUR MAN IN MOSCOW

Colonel Oleg Penkovskiy was an officer in Red Army Intelligence, the GRU, who passed strategic information to the British until he was caught, tried, and shot by the KGB. All of the information which he passed was important, some of it so important that it provided President Kennedy with the confidence to call Khrushchev's bluff in the Cuban missile crisis. This defection by a senior officer of GRU was MI6's most famous peacetime triumph.

Oleg Penkovskiy was a sensitive, introspective man, and a dedicated Communist for most of his life. According to all reports he never wavered in his ideological beliefs until he reached the rank which allowed him to move within the circles of the Soviet elite. There he first saw the immorality, drunkenness, and power-hungry behavior which his indoctrination had taught him could not possibly exist among Communist leaders. He was shocked. In Russia, this type of behavior is popularly associated with degenerate and decadent Western civilization. Penkovskiy, however, had visited the West and had not found it particularly decadent. Conversely, he seemed innocently to think that there was something remarkable about corruption in Soviet high places. Perhaps he thought only what he wished to think; perhaps he truly was naïve enough to think that corruption should be the province of a particular social system: whatever the faults in his reasoning, it turned him against Communism and started him on the way to becoming a British agent.

Oleg Penkovskiy was born in 1919 in the city of Ordzhonikidze. That same year his father was killed in the civil war, fighting as a White Russian against the Red Army. The boy Oleg received a typical Soviet education and was commissioned into an artillery regiment in 1939; shortly afterward he was accepted as a member of the Communist Party. During World War II he distinguished himself in combat and was decorated with the Orders of the Red Banner and the Red Star. In 1945 he returned to Moscow, married the daughter of a Soviet general, and continued his army career, specializing in intelligence. Eventually he was posted to the GRU where he served as an assistant military attaché in Ankara, Turkey.

It was at this point that Penkovskiy entered into the

rarefied atmosphere of the Soviet power structure. He had married into a top Russian family and held an important position in one of the country's two major intelligence establishments. His career seemed assured, but there was one blot on his record which both his own organization and the ferrets of the KGB seemed to have missed: his father had been a White Russian, a hated counterrevolutionary. In the whirligig of Russian life the political sins of the father are often visited on the son, but, for the moment, Penkovskiy was safe.

His term at the Ankara Embassy did not last long; he quarreled with his immediate superior and was sent back to Moscow. Surprisingly, this incident did not harm his career, for the quarrel was part of an interservice conflict between the KGB and the GRU. The incident actually endeared Penkovskiy at GRU headquarters and when he returned to Moscow it was to a promotion rather than punishment. He was made senior officer of the Chief Intelligence Directorate, a position which gave him access to many important military and state secrets. But he had scored a point off the KGB and, as Penkovskiy well knew, the KGB has a long memory.

In 1961 Penkovskiy decided to come over to the West. Three factors influenced his decision. The first was the venality which he had observed in the Kremlin, and which seems to have shocked him beyond proportion. He was also disillusioned with Communism on a political level, for he feared that Khrushchev's adventurous policies were leading the world toward nuclear war. Thirdly, on a more practical level, he was afraid that his personal security would be, or had already been, threatened by the discovery that his father had fought against the Revolution in 1919. Actually, this fact had not as yet been uncovered by his bosses, but Penkovskiy had every reason to fear their wrath when that unfortunate day arrived.

Penkovskiy's first effort to defect ended in failure. Moving cautiously, he tried to get in touch with the American intelligence officer operating in the American Embassy in Moscow. An offer to defect is a classic method of introducing a double agent into an enemy service, and the Americans were understandably reluctant to deal with him. In addition, they could not believe that a person in Penkovskiy's high position would be willing to turn traitor. Penkovskiy then tried the British, with better luck.

The British agent with whom Penkovskiy finally made his contact, and who was to serve as his liaison with the West throughout his career as a defector, was a Russian-speaking English engineer named Greville Wynne. Wynne specialized in trade with Russia and the East European countries, and in 1960 he organized the visit of the British Trade Delegation to Moscow. One of Penkovskiy's jobs at that time was to represent his government at the Delegation's exhibit, and it was there that he met Wynne and decided to approach him. Wynne, on his part, was later to claim that he was never a professional spy, and that in all his dealings with Penkovskiy he acted only as a patriotic Englishman trying to further the interests of his country. What seems more likely is that Wynne was involved in industrial espionage on behalf of England, a not inconsiderable intelligence operation, and that he caught a bigger fish than he had bargained for.

Wynne and Penkovskiy got to know each other quite well during the visit of the Trade Delegation, but the GRU colonel knew enough to proceed cautiously and it was not until the following year when Wynne returned to Moscow that Penkovskiy opened up to him. He told the Englishman that he had certain information which he wanted to convey to the West, and when Wynne left Moscow this time he carried with him an envelope from Penkovskiy addressed to the British Secret Service.

The information which Penkovskiy sent out with Wynne was designed only to establish his credentials with the West. Later that month Penkovskiy himself went to London at the head of a Soviet Trade Delegation. His job was twofold: to engage in industrial espionage and, as a member of the GRU, to watch the other members of the delegation. It was an ideal position for him to be in, for no one had the job of watching *him.* Therefore, it was not difficult for him to meet with Western intelligence officers on the morning of April 20 at the Mount Royal Hotel in London. The agents he met, two British and two American, had been greatly impressed with the information he had sent out with Wynne, and were even more delighted with the military documents he handed over that morning. They were so impressed that the two agencies involved—MI6 and the CIA—took every precaution to preserve their valuable defector. Penkovskiy was told to keep to his normal work schedule with the Trade Delegation during the day, while at night, with Wynne acting as intermediary, he was to meet with the four agents for a crash course in the technique of communicating with the West.

Of course the four agents—the Americans were known as Alexander and Oslaf, the British as Grille and Miles —realized that there was little about espionage technique in which they could instruct a colonel in the GRU. It was important, however, that he learn their radio procedures, and during those nights of secret meetings they reviewed an array of code signals and wavelength frequencies until Penkovskiy was letter-perfect. He was then given a long-range transistor radio on which he would receive his coded instructions, and a Minox miniature camera for use on secret documents. It was agreed that Wynne was to continue as liaison, and before Penkovskiy left for Moscow the deal was made. He would supply the two agencies with any material he felt vital to their interests; in return, should he be forced to flee the Soviet Union, he would be granted either British or American citizenship and would be given a position equal in rank to what he held in Russia.

Penkovskiy returned to Moscow irrevocably committed to the life of a traitor. To most men this would have meant a life of constant doubt and guilt, yet from his writings published after his death we know that Penkovskiy was assailed by neither of these nightmares.

He was that rarity among spies, a sincere man, and he firmly believed in the morality of what he was doing. He was privy to the secret Soviet preparations for nuclear war, and Khrushchev's threats to bombard the West filled him with horror. By normal standards he was a despicable traitor; by his standards he could do nothing else.

Whatever he was, traitor or idealist, he was good at it. When Greville Wynne next came to Moscow on business, Penkovskiy was waiting for him at the Sheremetyevo Airport. As they drove into town the Russian gave the Englishman a stack of military documents and a large number of rolls of exposed film. This was only the beginning. Throughout that summer Penkovskiy combed the GRU files assiduously, photographing all papers relating to Soviet rocketry and missile development. These he passed either directly to Wynne, who came to Moscow often during those months, or to other British contacts. One of the most unusual of these was the wife of a Western diplomat in Moscow. The routine was for the lady to sit on a bench in the Tsvetno Boulevard at a certain time with her children playing nearby. Penkovskiy, strolling by, would give one of the children a box of chocolates which the child would at once hand to its mother. The box, of course, contained rolls of film.

In addition to these contacts in Moscow, Penkovskiy made several trips to London during this period in his capacity as head of various Russian trade delegations. On each of these visits he met secretly with the British-American spy team and passed further information. Coincidentally, on one of these occasions the wife and daughter of General Serov, the head of GRU, were in London as tourists. The general asked Penkovskiy to look after his family while they were in London, and the colonel later described how he danced rock 'n' roll with young Svetlana Serov and took both mother and daughter sight-seeing around the city. Then, these social chores done, he would adjourn to an MI6 "safe house" for another session with his Western spy contacts.

During one of these visits he saw a chance to improve his image with Moscow, and took it. Karl Marx is buried in Highgate Cemetery in London, and Penkovskiy noticed that the grave of the Father of Communism was in a bad state of neglect, choked with weeds and apparently untended for years. Penkovskiy was still a Marxist, if not a Communist, and he was truly shocked. He sent off a strong protest to the first secretary of the Communist party in Moscow, and was later praised for his "socialist vigilance." The Soviet Embassy in London received a sharp note from home instructing that the master's grave be put in proper shape at once.

Late in September Penkovskiy went to Paris for the Soviet Industrial Fair, again meeting Wynne and passing along another batch of exposed film. This Paris meeting, however, was different from the ones in London and Moscow. Once again the four-man British-American team was present, once again they received Penkovskiy's material and praised him for his diligence, but this time they suggested that he defect permanently and not return to Moscow. This was an unusual action for an espionage controller to take. The controller is interested only in information; the safety of the agent is secondary. For the team to suggest that Penkovskiy defect while there was still valuable work for him to do in Moscow was contrary to normal procedure. But, they told the Russian, they felt that the game was almost up. By now the KGB had uncovered the story of Penkovskiy's White Russian father and this blot on his record was sure to cause a close investigation of *all* his activities. Besides that, no agent so highly placed could hope to avoid detection for long. The very quality of the information being passed would see to that. It was time for the balloon to go up and they urged Penkovskiy to return with them to England.

All this Penkovskiy knew; he was no newcomer to espionage. But he decided to return to Moscow. His motives are obscure. Perhaps he was concerned for the safety of his family; perhaps he felt it was his duty to return; perhaps, like many talented spies, he was compelled by ego to try for one more trip. All of these reasons would have been consistent with his character.

He lasted for more than just one trip, in fact he lasted for exactly one more year. It was an anxious, desperate year during which he passed an unusually large amount of information to Wynne and to other British contacts, and did so under the very noses of the KGB. But the Russian watchdogs were finally after him. The KGB people had long memories of the incident at Ankara, and the information about Penkovskiy's father gave them just the opening they wanted. They placed Penkovskiy under constant surveillance but, incredibly, the GRU colonel continued to get his information out. He must have been aware that the end was near, yet he continued to operate with a reckless fatalism. He seemed determined to hold out to the last, and even refused a British offer of escape by submarine through the Baltic Sea, a method which would have allowed him to save his family as well as himself.

At considerable risk, finally, Wynne came to Moscow to urge Penkovskiy to escape. The Russian refused and, completely disregarding his own safety, passed an additional set of films to his contact. Then, with arrest so near, he took care to get Wynne safely out of Russia. He used his authority to get the Englishman a place on a plane bound for Copenhagen, then returned to his Moscow apartment to await his fate.

Wynne left Moscow in July but it was not until October that Penkovskiy was arrested by the KGB. His gallant gesture in helping Wynne to escape proved to have been needless. The month after Penkovskiy was arrested, Wynne made an unwise trip to Budapest. There he was kidnapped by the KGB and taken to Lubianka Prison in Moscow to await trial with Penkovskiy.

The trial was the usual Soviet set piece. Both men pleaded guilty; Penkovskiy was sentenced to death, Wynne to eight years imprisonment. It was officially announced that Penkovskiy had been shot on the afternoon of May 15, 1963. Wynne served less than a year of his term. The following April he was exchanged for Soviet spy Gordon Lonsdale, following the pattern which had been established by the Abel-Powers swap.

Much of what we know about Oleg Penkovskiy comes from *The Penkovskiy Papers*, which was published after his death. The book purports to be Penkovskiy's memoirs, written late at night after his wife and family had gone to bed, and smuggled out of Russia several weeks before his arrest. It is largely an account of Penkovskiy's career in the GRU and contains a fascinating amount of information about Soviet Military Intelligence. Unfortunately, the authorship of the book is suspect. It seems inconceivable that Penkovskiy, a trained professional, would commit this sort of information to paper while under the surveillance of the KGB. Further, the book was purportedly translated from the Russian by Peter Deriabin, a KGB defector in the employ of the CIA, and edited by Frank Gibney, who also had been associated with Deriabin in the publication of *The Secret World* in 1959. No explanation has ever been given of how the papers were smuggled out of Russia and into Deriabin's hands.

Against this background, *The Penkovskiy Papers* is naturally suspect. It seems far more likely that the book was produced by the CIA as a weapon in the intelligence war; with the trusted team of Gibney and Deriabin as a front. During the thirty-seven days that they questioned Penkovskiy in London, the CIA and MI6 accumulated miles of tapes and transcripts. In addition, Penkovskiy confessed at his trial to having sent out of Russia over five thousand frames of film. It seems most probable that this was the material on which *The Penkovskiy Papers* was based.

7 SHOES FOR GALISHA

Throughout this narrative the name of Colonel Rudolf Abel appears with intriguing regularity. This one Russian, about whom so little is known, appears on the scene time and again, always playing some role in the major intelligence battles of the Cold War. At times his part is an important one, at other times he is no more than a supporting member of the cast, but rarely do we fail to see some sign of the ubiquitous colonel. Consider the following series of coincidences.

After Oleg Penkovskiy was shot as a spy, his English associate, Greville Wynne, was sentenced to eight years imprisonment and shipped to Vladimir Prison some ninety miles northeast of Moscow. There he was placed in the same cell which had been occupied by Francis Gary Powers, the U-2 pilot, during his stay there. Powers, of course, had been exchanged the year before for Colonel Abel in the first such transfer of spies. Wynne stayed at Vladimir Prison for less than one year. Then, in the second major exchange of espionage agents, he was brought to the Heerstrasse crossing point that leads into West Berlin and exchanged for Gordon Lonsdale, the KGB agent involved in Britain's Portland Naval Secrets case.

And who is Gordon Lonsdale? He is none other than Konon Trofimovich Molody, whom we last met serving as Abel's assistant in New York.

What we know of the early life of Konon Molody is both controversial and obscure. He was born in Moscow in 1922, but several different versions have been given of how he spent his first twenty years. All the versions, however, agree that during World War II he was a guerrilla fighter operating in German-occupied Russia. Posing as a peasant on his way to market, Molody made the mistake of going into town on a day when the Germans were rounding up men to be sent to a forced-labor camp. He was swept up in the draft, and would have been shipped out with the others but for the intervention of a German officer who ordered him freed. The "German" was a Russian agent who had infiltrated the Abwehr, or German Army Intelligence, and his name was Rudolf Abel. From that moment on Abel was Molody's lifelong hero. He was also Molody's mentor in the spy trade, and when Abel was sent to New York as *rezident*, he soon asked for Molody as his assistant. After five years with his chief in New York, Molody took the name of Gordon Lonsdale and went on to England to head his own network. There, in unconscious imitation of his master, he had his years of glory, was betrayed by a careless subordinate, was imprisoned, and eventually exchanged for a Western spy.

The conflicting stories concerning Lonsdale-Molody's early years are part of the war of words which intelligence establishments use to confuse and mislead each other. Both the KGB and the CIA have Departments of Misinformation whose sole purpose is to produce quantities of false material designed to confuse the enemy. *The Penkovskiy Papers* is a fine example of a CIA venture in this field. Lonsdale's memoirs, *Spy: Twenty Years of Secret Service*, is an equally good example of the Russian product. In his book, Lonsdale tells of his early years in an intriguing combination of half-truths and outright lies.

Lonsdale, as we shall call him, claims that he actually was born under that name in Cobalt, Ontario, the son of a Scots father and Finnish mother. His mother, he says, divorced his father and married another Finn. Then, goes the story, the happy little family left Canada in 1932 with the intention of returning to Finland, but by circumstances they ended up in Lvov, Poland. According to Lonsdale they lived there until that section of Poland was annexed by Russia at the beginning of World War II. At that point, he claims, he entered the Russian Secret Service.

Actually, there was a Gordon Lonsdale born in Cobalt, Ontario, in 1924, the son of a half-breed father and a Finnish mother. When his parents separated, young Lonsdale went with his mother back to her native Finland. There he died in 1940, just at the time of the Russo-Finnish War. The papers which established his Canadian birth came into the hands of Russian intelligence and were kept for future needs. Meanwhile, young Konon Molody, who was later to assume the name of Lonsdale, was living through an unhappy boyhood in Moscow. His father had died when the boy was seven years old and in the years following the Molody family lived on the edge of absolute poverty. In 1932 they were visited by Konon's Aunt Tatiana, who had emigrated to America and was now living in California. The aunt was shocked by the conditions in which the family was living and, as her contribution, suggested taking the boy back to America to live with her. Konon's mother readily agreed and sent off her son with Tatiana, who was able to get him out of Russia only by passing him off as her own child.

For six years Konon lived with his aunt in Berkeley, California. There he went to school and learned to speak English as well as he spoke Russian. Equally important, he absorbed the cultural background to go with the language; there would be no need for the Gaczyna school for this future agent. By the time he returned to Russia just before World War II he was fully qualified in the language and customs of the United States.

At this point fact and fiction flow together as Molody's cover story and the truth seem to coincide. During the early stages of the war he *was* in Lvov, Poland, and after the German invasion in 1941 he went underground and became a guerrilla fighter. It was then that his path first crossed that of Rudolf Abel.

From the very beginning of their relationship the two men respected and admired each other. The young Molody was deeply indebted to Abel and obviously worshiped him. Abel, in turn, was impressed by Molody's guerrilla exploits and his linguistic abilities. He at once marked him for a future role in the KGB, and years later, when the opportunity arose, asked for him to be sent to New York. The two men worked well together and Molody indicates in his memoirs that when he was ordered to London the team was broken up only after much reluctance and regret on both his part and Abel's. In retrospect this regret no doubt was genuine, for Molody's replacement as Abel's assistant was the bumbling drunkard, Reino Hayhanen, whose defection eventually led to Abel's arrest.

Sometime during that five-year stay in New York, Molody made a trip to Canada equipped with papers indicating that he was Gordon Arnold Lonsdale, born in Cobalt, Ontario, in 1924. What he needed was a verified copy of Lonsdale's birth certificate, which, in turn, could be used to get a Canadian passport in that name. He went to Cobalt, gave the name of Lonsdale, the date of birth, and the other particulars which the KGB had been so provident as to preserve. His information was good and he was confident that he could pass for the real Lonsdale, yet he later admitted to a few qualms as he stood at the registry counter and waited while the clerk looked through the files. Cobalt is a small town, and there was always the chance that someone passing through might hear the name and recall the young boy who had left for Finland years before. He had been taught that an outside chance can always defeat careful planning, and so he waited nervously, imagining a dozen possible disasters while the clerk took a lifetime to look through the files. But there was no disaster. Smiling, the clerk produced a photostat of the Lonsdale birth certificate and apologized for having kept Mr. Lonsdale waiting.

Once he had a copy of the birth certificate, obtaining a passport was a simple matter. All he needed was an application form, photographs, and the signatures of two sponsors. He had the pictures taken in a commercial studio and, for the sponsors, he simply picked two names out of the telephone directory and happily signed them to the form. On January 21, 1955, the Russian spy was issued a valid Canadian passport in the name of Gordon Lonsdale, the name under which he conducted his operations in England.

Gordon Lonsdale arrived in London in the spring of 1955 and established himself there in an unorthodox but effective manner. His procedure cannot be found in any handbook for spies; nevertheless it worked. Far from being a sly, secretive figure, Lonsdale exploded on the London scene as a popular character, a hard-living, hard-drinking ex-lumberjack from Canada. He let it be known to all who would listen that he had "made a pile of money" in some undisclosed venture, and had come over to the mother country looking for a business in which to invest it. He made friends quickly and soon established the reputation of being a gregarious type who was always good for a loan or a drink. In truth, this reputation was less a cover story than a personal preference. Lonsdale actually was a happy-go-lucky sort of person, and it was no effort for him to act the part. He possessed a sizable bank account; he ate well, drank well, owned a fine car, and kept a luxurious apartment at a fashionable address. Eventually this love of the good life was to help undo him, and when it finally happened it was not the first time that a Russian agent had succumbed to the temptations of a society he had been trained to despise.

But at this point in his career, Lonsdale was living high and loving every minute of it. As he told his newfound friends, he was in no hurry to find a business in which to invest; that would take care of itself. In the meantime he was enjoying himself and, like the well-trained KGB operative that he was, he was busy organizing his network.

The two most important members of this network were a married couple who went under the names of Peter and Helen Kroger. Although they were completely subordinate to Lonsdale's control in the network, they deserve more than our casual attention, for we have met them before under their true names of Morris and Lona Cohen. The Cohens were the two members of Yakovlev's American *rezidentura* who fled the country when the Rosenbergs were arrested. In America their lives had been undistinguished, as befitted two active espionage agents. Morris was a teacher in the New York City school system, and Lona seemed to be nothing more than a hardworking housewife. Everything about them was stamped with this brand of normalcy, even their political views, which, although decidedly left-wing, were not that much different from many other New York intellectuals and liberals. They had few friends, but those who knew them liked them. Lona was obviously an intelligent girl who had overcome a meager education with extensive reading; Morris was a well-qualified and popular teacher at Public School Number 86 in Manhattan. They seemed destined to live out these rather ordinary lives without change, but in 1950 the change came, and came abruptly. Without giving the customary one term's notice, Morris Cohen quit his job. To their friends, the Cohens announced that they were moving to California where Morris had a well-paying job as a Hollywood scriptwriter waiting for him. To these same friends it seemed like a dream come true, a little too good to be true—but before anyone could ask any questions the Cohens had vanished. They never went to California.

The reason for their disappearance is not difficult to guess. When the Rosenbergs were arrested, the Cohens knew that it was time for a change of scene. They closed their bank accounts, cashed their savings bonds, cleared their apartment of all incriminating documents, and disappeared.

Their move was well timed, for shortly after they left New York their names came to the attention of FBI agents investigating the Rosenberg case. The connection between the two families was slight—the Cohens and the Rosenbergs were known to have visited with each other and had attended some political functions together —but it was enough for the FBI to open a brief dossier on the one-time schoolteacher and his wife. Their fingerprints were obtained from army and civil defense records, and federal agents throughout the country were notified to report the whereabouts of the couple whenever they turned up.

They were never found and the Cohen dossier became one more file gathering dust in the offices of the FBI. Then, seven years later, something happened which made it urgent to find the Cohens. In June 1957 Colonel Rudolf Abel was arrested in New York. Among the papers found in his photographic studio appeared the names of Morris and Lona Cohen, as well as those of the Rosenbergs. There were even two passport photographs of the Cohens found in a wallet belonging to Abel. Now the FBI search for the Cohens became intense but the trail was cold and no amount of investigation could unearth any sign of the pair. They were long since gone from America and had long since shed the name of Cohen. By now they were living in a pleasant bungalow in Ruislip, England, under the names of Peter and Helen Kroger, and working actively in the espionage network headed by Gordon Lonsdale.

What happened to the Cohens between the time they

left New York and the time they arrived in England? We know that they went first to Australia, but how they traveled there is still a mystery. Equally a mystery is what they did in Australia for the next three years. It is unlikely that they engaged in any espionage work; their job was to lie low and wait. This appears to be confirmed by the statements made by the Russian defector Vladimir Petrov, who walked out of the Soviet Embassy in Canberra in 1954 with the records of every Russian agent operating in Australia. None of the cover names or descriptions fits the Cohens, and so we know nothing about their Australian sojourn except that they left there in 1953 on a roundabout journey that led to Vienna, Hong Kong, Tokyo, and, eventually, Moscow. There they were briefed by Center on their new assignment in England. They were provided with an array of forged Canadian and New Zealand passports in various names, but their permanent cover name was to be Kroger. By the end of 1954 they were in England, just two months before their superior, Gordon Lonsdale, was due to arrive from Canada. They rented the house in Ruislip, and mild-mannered, scholarly Peter Kroger opened a bookshop in London as a cover occupation.

The Krogers settled in quickly. They made new friends, minded their own business, and, in fact, began to live very much the same kind of life that the Cohens had lived in New York. They were about to embark on the most important task in their espionage careers, and only a few minor characters were needed to complete the cast and set the stage.

The occupation which Gordon Lonsdale chose for his cover could not have been more different than that picked by the respectable bookseller, Peter Kroger. Lonsdale went into the jukebox and gum-vending machine trade, a business usually associated with minor hoodlums and other shady characters. People who subsequently learned the true nature of Lonsdale's profession were baffled by this apparently absurd cover story, yet on reflection it made a certain kind of sense. The nature of the business allowed Lonsdale to travel freely and without suspicion throughout Europe, and it is quite likely that he derived a personal pleasure out of making money from what he considered symbols of capitalistic decadence. Not that there was much money to be made. The business was almost profitless for him, but it served its purpose as a cover and gave a fairly presentable reason for Lonsdale's almost unlimited funds. But more than anything else, the jukebox business gave Lonsdale an opportunity to operate in the semi-legitimate world of London's "wide boys." For a man whose love of danger was almost pathological, this was reason enough.

With his cover story set, Lonsdale was now ready to begin operations. He decided on the Krogers' cottage at Ruislip as the headquarters for the ring, and the house was soon furnished with all the modern paraphernalia of espionage. In the loft of the bungalow Lonsdale installed a fifty-yard aerial, and headphones with wires leading to the radio which was concealed below a trapdoor in the kitchen. The radio was fitted with the special keying device for high-speed transmission which meant that broadcasts never had to last more than thirty seconds at a time. The location of the house had been chosen with care. Only a few miles away was the U.S. Air Force base at South Ruislip where a tremendous amount of ground-to-air radio communication took place daily. This virtually ensured against the detection of the Kroger transmitter, which operated only briefly against the background of innumerable other signals.

Other sophisticated equipment at the Ruislip cottage included a shortwave receiver with a special headset for listening to high-frequency bands; the inevitable miniature camera; a microdot reader concealed within a box of Yardley face powder; a hollow Ronson lighter used to store microfilm negatives; hollow flashlight batteries; and a hip flask with a secret compartment containing iron oxide, which was used to show up Morse code messages on magnetic tape. Also secreted about the house was more than $20,000 in "getaway" money, and seven passports in alternate cover names. Lonsdale and the Krogers were ready for business. Now all they needed was the information to pass.

An elaborate spy network is rarely intruded into a target country with a specific mission in mind. Usually the network exists in order to gather all sorts of information which might be of interest to Center. In the case of the Lonsdale-Kroger setup, however, a specific project was involved. Lonsdale's mission was to discover the secrets of Britain's new submarine defenses. At that time Russia was building a large submarine fleet and Soviet technicians were anxious to know what anti-submarine weap-

ons were being developed by the West. They knew that
the British had been successful in perfecting new asdic
and sonar devices at the secret Admiralty Weapons
Establishment at Portland, and Lonsdale was given the
job of getting the information.

It is one of the ironies of espionage work that the
weakest link in the chain is always the agent in the
field, the man who takes the most chances and the one
who is most likely to crack. The *rezident* may sit in his
lofty position and control the operation with consummate
skill; the cut-outs, in this case the Krogers, may perform
their technical work perfectly; but unless the agent in the
field develops the information, the elaborate network is
nothing more than an expensive failure. And the agent,
upon whom all this depends, is generally either an
idealist—and such a type can change his beliefs at any
moment—or a person of flawed character: a drunkard,
a dope addict, a homosexual, a womanizer, or some
form of social misfit who can be blackmailed into
working against the interests of his country. That
all of the high-powered technology of an industrial society, all the careful planning, the codes, the sophisticated equipment—that all of this should ultimately come
to rest upon the efforts of grubby little men with grubby
little secrets is the final irony of espionage.

Lonsdale's man inside the Portland Naval Establishment was Harry Frederick Houghton, a former naval
master-at-arms now working as a clerk in the Underwater Weapons Establishment. Houghton had come to
the attention of the KGB when he was a member of the

staff of the naval attaché at the British Embassy in Warsaw. Houghton was a heavy drinker who needed much more money than he could ever hope to earn in order to supply his habit. He was a notorious character in the Warsaw diplomatic community. He drank, he broke his wife's leg during an argument, he played the black market, and he had several affairs with Polish girls. This marked him as a prime prospect for the Russians.

Houghton did not last long in Warsaw. Because of his escapades he was soon sent back to England where, in an amazing decision, the admiralty decided that he would do less harm to Her Majesty's interests if he were to be transferred to the top-secret Underwater Weapons Testing Establishment at Portland. The decision can only be regarded as a stupendous blunder, comparable to the one the KGB made when it sent the alcoholic Reino Hayhanen to New York as Rudolf Abel's assistant. But the decision was made, Houghton went to work at Portland, and Lonsdale had his grubby little man.

He had his grubby little woman, too. Ethel Gee was a fortyish spinster who worked side by side with Harry Houghton at the Underwater Weapons Establishment. Ethel did not have the stuff of which spies are made, but she had the bad luck and questionable taste to fall in love with Houghton and thus become the final member of the Lonsdale network. Her motives for spying were never ideological. Houghton told her what to do, and she did it. In the process she did nicely for herself, and at the time of her arrest had managed to accumulate £6000, which she accounted for by claiming that she had saved it out of her salary of £500 per year. The mathematics worked against her.

The acquisition of Ethel Gee by the network was a fortunate stroke. Houghton was soon transferred to the Fleet Report Unit at Portland, a much less sensitive position, but with Ethel on the job the flow of information continued from the Underwater Weapons Establishment. The information passed from Ethel to Houghton to Lonsdale. The *rezident* then selected the material to be transmitted, enciphered it, and passed it along to the Krogers for dispatch to Moscow Center. The operation was an unquestioned success. The specific information which Center had demanded was produced soon after the operation began, and within a short time the Russian Navy knew all they had to know about the British anti-submarine defenses. Lonsdale was commended by Center and told to continue the good work. The net continued to operate and Lonsdale had every reason to be proud of having engineered a major espionage coup.

In his memoirs, which were published after his exchange for Greville Wynne, Lonsdale makes no secret of his dislike for Harry Houghton. In fact, he blames the hard-drinking former sailor for the dissolution of his network. His resentment of Houghton comes out clearly in the book; it is the resentment of a professional forced to work with an amateur.

The downfall of Harry Houghton began not so much because of his drinking but because of his unpopularity at the Underwater Weapons Establishment. Houghton was a bitter, sarcastic man, one who made enemies, not friends. Because of this unpopularity the Establishment finally managed to get him transferred to the Fleet Report Unit after months of protest to the Civil Service commissioners. Again, his unpopularity caused the dock police at the Naval Base to keep a suspicious eye on his movements. They noticed when he bought an expensive car; they noticed when he bought a house and furnished it luxuriously; the noticed the costly gifts he gave to Ethel Gee; and they noticed the nightly round that Houghton made of the Portland pubs, spending more money on drink than the total of his salary. When the local security authorities totaled it all up they knew that they had a case for MI5.

Once Houghton and Gee were placed under MI5 surveillance it was only a matter of time before the trail of the two amateur spies led directly to the door of the *rezident.* MI5 agents followed Houghton on his trips to London and observed him giving packages to Lonsdale during apparently accidental meetings. Lonsdale, in turn, was closely watched and he soon led the agents to the Krogers' bungalow at Ruislip. The surveillance went on for several months, following the MI5 maxim that no arrests should ever be made until everyone in the network is identified. Of course, this resulted in additional information being transmitted to Moscow Center, but the situation was allowed to continue in order to ensure a clean sweep once the spies were arrested.

MI5 used the full range of its services during the Lonsdale investigation. Agents posed as painters, porters, street cleaners, electricians, and book salesmen in order to keep the network under observation. Female agents posing as working bachelor girls took the apartment next to Lonsdale's and installed high-powered listening devices in the walls. When Lonsdale took one of his periodic trips abroad he deposited a suitcase at his bank. MI5 agents obtained a search warrant and examined the suitcase in his absence. Among other things they found a hollow table lighter in which were signal plans for monitoring incoming Russian radio transmissions. Finally, when the weight of the evidence seemed sufficient, MI5 notified the Special Branch at Scotland Yard and asked for an arrest.

Lonsdale, Houghton, and Gee were arrested in a London street as they were exchanging bundles of Admiralty papers disguised as grocery parcels. All three were taken to Scotland Yard, and the manner in which they reacted to questioning was indicative of the broad gulf between the amateur and the professional.

Houghton, in a state of shock, blurted out, "I have been a bloody fool."

Ethel Gee's first statement was both naïve and astonishing. She simply said, "I have done nothing wrong."

Lonsdale was questioned by the head of the Special Branch, Superintendent Smith. Relaxed and cynical, the Russian agent sat back in his chair and said, "To any question you might ask me, my answer is 'No,' so you needn't trouble to ask." Superintendent Smith asked his questions anyway, but Lonsdale only smiled briefly and shook his head, thus beginning a period of silence which was to last until the final day of his trial.

Superintendent Smith left the silent Lonsdale in custody and drove with a small force of men to the quiet cottage at Ruislip. The Krogers, too, were professionals. They showed no alarm when told that they were under arrest. It was all a mistake, they told the chief of Special Branch, but mistakes will happen and they assured him of their willingness to cooperate. When told that they would have to come along right then and there, Mrs. Kroger nodded understandingly. She put on her coat, picked up her handbag, and announced that she was ready to go. As an afterthought, she added, "As I am going out for some time, may I go and stoke the boiler?"

Superintendent Smith was equally understanding. "Certainly," he said, "but first let me see what you've got in that handbag."

Mrs. Kroger refused, and had to be forced to give it up. Her reluctance was understandable. From inside the flap of the brown leather bag the Superintendent took a plain white envelope. In it were a six-page letter in Russian, a glass slide holding three microdots, and a typed sheet of cipher.

"You can go and stoke the boiler now, if you wish," said Smith politely, but Mrs. Kroger had lost all interest in that domestic chore.

Aside from being incriminating, the contents of the envelope cast an interesting light on the private life of a spy. The typed sheet of cipher turned out to be a routine message to Moscow Center, but the microdots, when enlarged, were found to be three personal letters to Lonsdale from his family, and the six-page letter in Russian was his reply. Even a spy has a private life; even a spy has to worry about shopping for his wife and must listen to complaints about the high cost of living back home.

The first letter was from Lonsdale's Russian wife, Galisha, and was dated November 13, 1960. The other two were dated in December, one from Galisha and one from Lonsdale's daughter, Dema. The letters were typical of the type that women write to their men during long separations: a mixture of chatty gossip, self-pity, and news from home. From the way the letters were written it was clear that Galisha did not fully understand the nature of her husband's job. She obviously knew that he was engaged in clandestine work but she did not know where. From her attitude, her husband could just as easily have been an important Embassy official in some far-off capital. This was made abundantly clear in the first letter, in which Galisha told her husband that his mother was desperately ill.

"I am writing to tell you the truth so you should know that you must somehow make haste to come home—after all, one has only one mother in this world."

As if Lonsdale could simply drop everything and hurry home to Moscow. Galisha had a way of mixing sad news with mundane matters, for in the next sentence she says, "In spite of my unhappy mood, I must ask you if it is possible to send me a white brocade dress and a pair of white shoes."

Galisha opened her second letter in the approved form

for a citizen of a Soviet republic: "Hello my darling. I congratulate you on the past 43rd anniversary of the October Revolution. We were expecting letters from you but it turned out they may come at the end of the month. . . . On November 3rd we had an evening party and I sang. It reminded me of our life in Prague and I felt very sad. . . . We all were deeply sorry you were not with us, and so was I especially. If my memory does not deceive me it is already seven Octobers and six May Day celebrations that I am alone. . . . How unjust life is. I fully understand you are working and this is your duty, and you love your work and try to do all this very conscientiously. Nevertheless my reasoning is somehow narrow-minded in a female fashion and I suffer dreadfully. Write to me how you feel and write to me how you love me and maybe I will feel better."

Then once again in that odd mixture of sorrow and practicality, Galisha asked for an increase in her allowance: "If possible please let me have 2500 roubles a month."

These letters from his wife told MI5 a great deal about Lonsdale. The very fact that they were forwarded at all showed that Moscow Center considered him an important agent and a man to be kept happy at all costs. For minor agents, Center would never add to the chances of defection by forwarding letters from home.

Lonsdale's answer also gave valuable information to the experts at MI5.

"My beloved Galisha. Just received your mail. I am very happy to have three letters from you in one lot. . . .

I will write this very day to V.M. that 2500 roubles should be handed over to you, or more correctly, 250 roubles. [Russia had just undergone a currency change. One new ruble equaled ten old rubles.] A few days ago I saw photographs of the new currency. To me it is a considerable improvement. . . . About the white brocade dress, it is a very difficult matter. In 'other countries' brocade is not worn. How to send it to you and when? A dress and shoes cannot be put in a pocket."

Later in the letter Lonsdale, too, bemoaned their separation. "I understand you quite well. You wrote that seven October anniversaries were celebrated without me. [This apparently refers to the anniversary of the Russian Revolution and not to any personal anniversary.] This is so, of course. But I have celebrated them without you and without the children and my people. When we were in Prague I tried to explain everything to you. I am not complaining, but even you cannot imagine how sad I feel in general, and especially at this moment. . . . Such is life. . . . I know this expression in so many languages I feel sick."

And later in this long, sad letter: "I do know what loneliness is. From the age of ten, during the past twenty-nine years, I have spent only ten years with my own people. I did not wish it and I did not seek it, but so it turned out to be. It did not depend on me. I have thought very much about it—why all this? The answer is it all started as far back as 1932 when mother decided to dispatch me to the nether regions [i.e., California]. At that time she could not imagine, of course, all the consequences of this step and I do not blame her."

And in a postscript to the letter: "I will be thirty-nine shortly. Is there much left?"

This postscript was a damaging mistake. The real Gordon Lonsdale would have only been thirty-six that year. It was Konon Molody who would be thirty-nine.

Here was a picture of the lonely life of the spy, stripped bare of all the claptrap of espionage fiction. According to Lonsdale he had been a spy in the service of his country for almost twenty years, and he had performed his job with pride and dedication. But the burden was becoming harder to bear as the years went by. He was alone and he could never relax. Every move he made was a calculated act; every word he spoke had to be carefully considered; every step he took was a journey into enemy territory. It is a terrifying type of life to contemplate and, regardless of their nationality, it is difficult not to sympathize with those who lead it.

In March 1961, all five defendants in the Portland Naval Secrets case were tried at the Old Bailey court before Lord Parker, the Lord Chief Justice of England. They were charged with conspiracy to commit espionage. They were brought to trial for this particular offense for two reasons. If they had been charged with spying under the Official Secrets Act the maximum sentence which could have been passed would have been fourteen years. The second reason for not proceeding under the Official Secrets Act was that under the conspiracy charge MI5 agents would not have to give evidence and thus reveal counterespionage techniques.

All five pleaded not guilty, but the weight of the

evidence was such that the verdict was never in doubt. Lonsdale made a favorable impression in court, particularly on the last day of the trial. Seeing that he himself was doomed, he asked for permission to take the stand, where he made a statement in which he attempted to exonerate the Krogers of all complicity. Of course, he could not say in plain words that he was a Russian spy, but by implicitly admitting the nature of his operations he felt he might be able to save the two most valuable members of his network. This was the way he put it:

"I have known the Krogers since 1955. During the last two or three years I often visited them, and sometimes spent weekends at their home. Whenever they went away from Ruislip, Peter Kroger would leave the keys with me, and ask me to stay at his house, where he had antiquarian books worth several thousand pounds. He knew that I lived in a very small service flat where the staff had passkeys. I used this as an excuse to keep at the Krogers' house some of my property—for example, my Praktina camera, various photographic equipment, and some other articles.

"In July last year, I gave Mr. Kroger as a birthday present a cigarette lighter and a pair of wooden bookends which appear to be ordinary household articles. As you have seen, these articles have secret compartments which contain various objects produced here as exhibits. Even a cursory examination would show that the signal plans found there were a reserve duplicate set of plans found at my flat. In short, I want to make it clear that the following exhibits either belong to me or were given by me to the Krogers: the Ronson lighter, the microscope, the flask, the flashlight, the tin of talcum, and several pieces of paper, and 2563 U.S. dollars found in the attic.

"At one time when the Krogers were away, I constructed the hiding place found in the foundations of the house, and deposited there for long-term storage the radio transmitter and other articles. I took great care that no traces of its existence were left. I knew if the contents of the hiding place were discovered it would land Mr. and Mrs. Kroger in very serious trouble."

Lonsdale ended his statement by saying: "I realize it is too late to make amends now, but I feel the least I can do in the circumstances is to accept full responsibility for my actions, irrespective of the consequences to me personally."

It was a brilliant performance, and as Lonsdale calmly folded his notes and walked back to his seat, there were many in the courtroom who would have liked to applaud. But the Lord Chief Justice of England was less impressed than were the spectators who crowded the courtroom that day. Lonsdale was sentenced to twenty-five years imprisonment; the Krogers, despite his efforts, to twenty years; and Houghton and Ethel Gee to fifteen years. But it was less than three years later that Konon Trofimovich Molody was exchanged for Greville Wynne at the Heerstrasse crossing point in West Berlin, and one might almost hope that before he went over the border he found time to buy a white brocade dress and a pair of shoes for Galisha.

8 THE TAIL THAT WAGGED THE DOG

In the looking-glass world of international diplomacy, intelligence, and espionage, the Central Intelligence Agency of the United States stands alone in the West, a mammoth organization equaled only by its Russian counterpart, the KGB. That this giant of Western intelligence should be American is one indication of how far the country has come since the innocent days after World War I, when Henry L. Stimson disbanded the State Department's "Black Chamber" intelligence unit with the admonition that "gentlemen don't read other people's mail."

As ludicrous as it may seem today, this innocent attitude characterized most American intelligence operations, such as they were, throughout the period between the two World Wars. In a sense it may even be said that this attitude was responsible for the eventual birth of the CIA, for the CIA exists today because of Pearl Harbor. The sneak Japanese attack in 1941 which destroyed our Pacific Fleet carried a lesson with it which the nation was quick to learn. Investigation after the attack showed that the country should never have been caught by surprise, that ample information of what the Japanese were up to existed before the attack, and that this information should have been used to alert our military commanders in the Pacific.

This information was made available to the American government literally by MAGIC, for that was the code word used by the State Department to cover the activities of a small group of cryptographers who managed to break the Japanese diplomatic code in the days just before the beginning of World War II. After years of experimentation the code breakers constructed an exact duplicate of the Japanese enciphering machine. That too was called MAGIC, and magic it was, for it gave American military and government leaders the privilege of reading the daily communications between the Japanese Foreign Office and its ambassadors throughout the world.

In November 1941, with Europe in flames, the attention of the world was focused on Washington, D.C., where Japanese ambassadors Kurusu and Nomura had for several weeks been engaged in negotiations with the United States government. Although World War II was two years old, both Japan and America were still neutrals, and the apparent purpose of the Washington meetings was to maintain that neutrality and to settle the differences between the two countries by diplomatic means. The second purpose of the meetings, which was not apparent to anyone but the Japanese, was to delay negotiations long enough for Japan to mount her long-planned air and sea attacks on the American installations at Pearl Harbor and in the Philippines.

Because of MAGIC, the American leaders knew Japan's diplomatic moves in advance. They also knew what type of information Japanese agents were collecting, where certain Fleet units had been ordered, and even which code word would be used to signal a declaration of war. Yet all this information did not save the United States from being surprised.

In the final days before Pearl Harbor, the MAGIC people intercepted and decoded four last-minute signals addressed to the Japanese ambassadors in Washington. The first signal simply said that an extremely long message would be sent in fourteen parts on the following day. However, some of the wording in the signal was significant, for the ambassador was told: "The situation is extremely delicate, and when you receive it [the fourteen-part signal] I want you to please keep it secret for the time being."

The fourteen-part signal was intercepted the following day, December 6, by the U.S. Navy monitoring station on Bainbridge Island near Seattle. The first thirteen parts turned out to be nothing more than a restatement of the Japanese viewpoint on Pacific problems—all of which had been repeated endlessly at the Washington meetings. Only the last part contained new information, but it was startling news. Japan was suddenly breaking off the talks: "The Japanese government regrets to have to notify hereby the American government that in view of the attitude of the American government it cannot but consider that it is impossible to reach an agreement through further negotiations."

The third message, Tokyo Number 907, was cloaked in ambiguous language, but we now know that it set the time for the attack on Pearl Harbor and instructed Ambassador Kurusu to deliver a declaration of war.

"Will the ambassador please submit to the United States government (if possible to the Secretary of State) our reply to the United States at 1 P.M. on the 7th, your time."

At 5 A.M. on December 7, the final message was intercepted by the Navy. It read: "After deciphering part 14 of my #902, and also #907, #908, and #909, please destroy at once the remaining cipher machine and all machine codes. Dispose in like manner also secret documents."

In retrospect it is difficult to see how Pearl Harbor could have occurred with this information in the hands of the American military leaders. The MAGIC messages did not say literally: "Air raid on Pearl Harbor next Sunday," but they did give every indication of hostile action by the Japanese, coinciding with a rupture in diplomatic relations. In the world of international politics, the addition of these two factors has to equal war.

A full-scale military alert was the least possible reaction. Yet when the Japanese bombs rained down on the ships and men at Pearl Harbor that Sunday they fell on an American military machine caught completely by surprise.

Why did this happen? Was the information disregarded? Were the admirals and generals negligent?

Subsequent investigations did show some negligence by high-ranking officers, but the main reason that MAGIC failed was that in 1941 there did not exist in America a single, central organization equipped to analyze and evaluate intelligence information. Had such an organization existed, the unmistakable meaning of the MAGIC messages would have been transmitted to the right people at the right time. It was an expensive lesson to learn, but a valuable one. Immediately after Pearl Harbor, President Franklin D. Roosevelt created the nation's first central espionage agency, the Office of Strategic Services.

The OSS, under the wartime command of General "Wild Bill" Donovan, operated in the swashbuckling manner of cloak-and-dagger espionage. Most of the agency's activities were overt acts of sabotage and guerrilla training. OSS agents parachuted behind the enemy lines to meet with Resistance leaders, plan campaigns, and supply them with a fantastic variety of weapons gadgetry. Division 19, a special weapons section, was established under the direction of Dr. H. M. Chadwell to supply the range of ingenious arms needed by the anti-Nazi underground in Europe, and the weaponry produced would have made even James Bond envious, had he been around at the time.

One of the first weapons in the OSS arsenal was an incendiary bomb in the shape of a small book. The celluloid casing was filled with napalm jelly fused to an ignition timer which could be set for periods of up to three days. Another was an explosive charge nicknamed "Casey Jones" because it was designed for railroad sabotage. Casey Jones was simply a steel box containing a charge of TNT inside and a permanent magnet on top. The box could be easily placed on the underside of a locomotive. The function of Casey Jones was to derail trains—but not just any trains. To get the maximum value out of a derailment, the OSS decided that the explosion should occur in a tunnel, thereby blocking rail traffic for a maximum period of time. So Casey Jones was fitted with an electric eye, a special one developed by Bell Laboratories, which was not affected by a slow absence of light, such as sunset, but only by a sharp cutting off of light—such as when a train entered a tunnel. Then Casey Jones went to work. And just to make sure that no overenthusiastic railroad worker tampered with the device, a sign in German was placed on the box which read: "Removal strictly forbidden under heaviest penalties. Heil Hitler."

Other OSS devices included a silent, flashless pistol for night raiders, a submachine gun with the same virtues, an explosive charge in the shape of a piece of coal which could be casually tossed onto the pile in a locomotive, and a simple device called "Hedy" to be used by agents in tight situations. Hedy was nothing more than a firecracker and a whistle combined, activated by pulling a small wire loop. It was designed to produce a diversionary effect. Trapped in a place like a crowded hotel lobby, the agent simply pulled the loop and let Hedy get to work. The result was a high-pitched screech that simulated perfectly the sound of a falling bomb—followed by a deafening roar. All completely harmless, but in the resulting confusion more than one OSS agent managed to make his escape.

Not all the fancy OSS weapons were that successful; one died aborning because it was *too* successful. The OSS was asked to provide a hand grenade for American agents which would be less clumsy to handle than the conventional Mills grenade. The technicians working on the project decided, logically enough, that a grenade which exploded on contact would be ideal, and that since every American boy knows how to handle a baseball, that would be the ideal shape. The weapon was developed with customary OSS dispatch and sent for testing to the Aberdeen Proving Grounds of the U.S. Army Ordnance. Army and OSS officers gathered to watch the demonstration of the weapon by a civilian engineer who, they assumed, had been thoroughly briefed. The engineer told the assembled brass that the new grenade was ideal in its simplicity since it could be handled like any baseball. To prove the point he tossed it high in the air. This, of course, armed the grenade. When it came down he caught it like an experienced outfielder —and was blown to bits. In the horror of the aftermath the OSS canceled the project.

But these dramatic devices, and the exploits of in-

dividual OSS agents—although they contributed materi-
ally to the winning of the war—were only a small part
of the purpose for which the organization was founded.
What was needed was a central intelligence clearing
house, and in the last year of the war General Donovan
suggested that the OSS begin to assume such functions.
The government agreed, but it was not until September
1947 that the Central Intelligence Agency came into
being. By that time the OSS had been disbanded and
the new agency was forced to start from scratch, organizing with the help of former OSS members and the
sometimes overenthusiastic help of army and navy intelligence units. The latter, as might be expected, were
not overjoyed by the creation of a single, supreme intelligence agency. But the CIA was an established fact,
created by act of Congress, and so the other agencies
proceeded on the venerable American maxim that "if
you can't beat 'em, join 'em," and tried to move as many
of their members as possible into the fledgling organization.

Among those who attended the birth of the CIA was
Allen Dulles, who had been the top OSS representative
in Switzerland during the war. After the war he returned to private life and the practice of law, but this
did not prevent him from playing an active role in
formulating the legislation that created the CIA. The
following year he headed a committee of three which
was asked to report to President Truman on the effec-
tiveness of the CIA and the relationship of the new organization to the other intelligence organs within the
government.

In his report Dulles recommended that the CIA should have complete internal control of its staff and personnel, and that it should have sole responsibility for American intelligence activities. To balance this very powerful position, he also suggested that the CIA should have nothing to do with the making of policy, its job being limited to the collection and analysis of hard intelligence. These powers and limitations were duly incorporated into the charter of the CIA. They have often been departed from and, ironically, most often during those nine years when Dulles himself was director of the organization.

Allen Dulles became director of the CIA in 1953. At the same time his brother, John Foster Dulles, was Secretary of State to President Dwight Eisenhower. Between them the two brothers wielded a disproportionate amount of influence on national policy, and it was during Dulles's directorship that the CIA grew to its present position of power. Far from confining itself to the gathering of hard intelligence, the agency became actively involved in diplomatic and political maneuvering. It organized the Iranian coup which overthrew the government of the anti-American Premier Mossadegh; in 1954 it overthrew the Communist-dominated government of President Arbenz in Guatemala; in 1961 it played a major role in the abortive revolt of the French generals in Algeria; and throughout the troubled times in the Congo it maintained what amounted to a private army and air force which opposed the Communist elements there. In later years it was responsible for the attempt to overthrow the Castro government in Cuba which ended in the Bay of Pigs disaster, and it was the CIA which recommended to President Johnson that troops be sent to the Dominican Republic. All of these actions were contrary to the stated purpose of the CIA, but it was typical of the climate of the times that the majority of the American people simply applauded the successful operations and deplored the fiascos.

Defenders of the CIA base their defense on the National Security Act under which the agency was created. In that act it is stated that the CIA shall not only collect and evaluate intelligence, but that it shall "perform such other functions and duties related to Intelligence affecting the national security as the National Security Council may from time to time direct." Critics of the CIA complain that it is under this "blank check" clause that the agency interferes in the internal affairs of other countries, even to the extent of toppling, or attempting to topple, governments. The CIA, however, has grown to such size that effective criticism is difficult. The congressional committee which oversees the activities of the agency is generally peopled with CIA sympathizers, and efforts to expand the committee have been continually rebuffed. The only effective control over the CIA rests in the National Security Council, which, in effect, means the President of the United States. Thus the CIA is in many ways the creature of the political party in power.

One of the beneficial results of the CIA's Bay of Pigs adventure in Cuba was the creation of the President's Foreign Intelligence Board. Most critics of the Cuban disaster felt that it was due in great part to the lack of an independent judgment of the CIA's intelligence estimates. In creating the Board, the then President John Kennedy made it a continuing body with instructions to report to the President every six months on the competence of the CIA. In addition, Kennedy appointed a special committee to recommend what steps should be taken to avoid another Cuba. In its report the committee noted two criticisms of CIA operations which had been voiced before. The first was that its leaders continually preferred to believe CIA intelligence estimates evn in the face of overwhelming contradictory evidence gathered by other agencies. The second was that the CIA was simply not equipped to engage in military adventures. As a result, the committee offered two major recommendations:

1. That the CIA should have no *operational* role (as opposed to planning) in any future engagement similar to Cuba. The agency, however, was to continue its small-scale covert operations.

2. That a new position be created, that of Director of National Intelligence. This official would serve directly under the President at the level of the National Security Council. His job would be to supervise and evaluate the intelligence gathered by the CIA and the military services.

Kennedy accepted the first recommendation, but nothing was ever done about the second.

The final change in the American intelligence community came in 1965 with the reorganization of the U. S. Intelligence Board, the body which reviews the entire range of the nation's intelligence activities. With the reorganization was created the Defense Intelligence Agency to coordinate all the intelligence requirements coming out of the Pentagon. Prior to the creation of the DIA there were six military representatives from three different echelons as members of the board. The reorganization streamlined the board, but it is still a complex organism. It is headed by the President of the United States, under whom is the National Security Council, and then the Director of Central Intelligence. Under the director, who reports directly to the President, are the following members:

Deputy Director of CIA reporting to Director of CIA.

Director of the DIA reporting to the Joint Chiefs of Staff.

Assistant to Secretary of State reporting to the Secretary of State.

Director of the National Security Agency reporting to the Assistant Secretary of Defense.

Observer for the FBI reporting to the Director of the FBI.

Observer for the Atomic Energy Commission reporting to the Director of the Atomic Energy Commission.

Assistant Army Chief of Staff for Intelligence reporting to the Army Chief of Staff.

Director of Naval Intelligence reporting to the Chief of Naval Operations.

Assistant Air Chief of Staff for Intelligence reporting to the Air Force Chief of Staff.

The headquarters of the CIA is situated on one hundred and forty acres of land in the township of Langley, Virginia, only twenty minutes by car from the center of

Washington, D.C. The headquarters building itself is huge, covering nine acres, with twenty-one acres of adjoining parking lots. The number of people who work at Langley is secret, but most estimates put it at around ten thousand, which is almost as many as the number of people who work at the State Department. In addition, a part of the CIA's staff is housed in a complex of buildings in the surburban section of Washington. These buildings were the original headquarters of the CIA, and from them little blue buses ferry passengers and messages to the White House, the Pentagon, and the new headquarters at Langley.

Employees of the CIA are divided into two categories: the "blacks" and the "whites," and it has nothing to do with their skin color. The blacks are covert operators, involved in clandestine operations, and their connection with the agency is always concealed. The whites are overt employees, openly acknowledged by the CIA, and tend to be researchers and technicians. Both blacks and whites are screened before employment and are recruited, to a great degree, from the upper scholastic ten percent of the nation's colleges and universities. Many college professors are former officers of the CIA, the OSS, or Army Intelligence, and they regularly look over their classes for prospective CIA material.

Because of this the CIA always has many more applicants than it can accept: the maximum number accepted each year is one hundred. Out of each thousand persons who apply, eighty percent are at once screened out because of insufficient education or unsuitable background. The twenty percent remaining go through a second screening which eliminates eleven percent because of unfavorable personal characteristics. Of the nine percent remaining, four percent are then screened out for security reasons, such as having relatives in Communist-controlled countries. Those who survive this triple screening form the body of recruits who go to work each year for the CIA.

Just as in the British Secret Service, wealth and family background count in the CIA. CIA recruiters, rather defensively, like to point out that the majority of their employees are graduates of non-Ivy League colleges. On the other hand, they concede that the top twenty men in the agency *are* both Ivy and wealthy, and that a list of the distinguished persons who have taken part in CIA cover activities would read like a roster of the top clubs in New York, Philadelphia, and Boston. Some of the most respected law firms, trust funds, and banks in the country have been used to cover CIA operations and to channel CIA funds. In fact, in 1948 when the CIA was seeking new ways to mount covert operations in peacetime, it turned for funds not to the Congress of the United States, but preferred to pass the hat among wealthy friends at the Brook Club in New York. This preference for the informal, this dependence on the nation's elite, is characteristic of both the CIA and the British Secret Service. The British, however, have been at the business a lot longer and many a CIA official must look with longing at the MI6 setup where the Old Boys run the intelligence system as they see fit and use the Official Secrets Act to avoid public scrutiny.

One of the strongest criticisms mounted against the CIA has been over its secret involvement in the academic community. The first indication of this involvement came to public notice in 1966 when *Ramparts* magazine disclosed that Michigan State University had provided academic cover for a CIA-sponsored police operation in South Vietnam from 1955 to 1959. The magazine reported that the university ran a police training program under a $25 million contract, and also that five CIA agents had been intruded into the program with the knowledge of university officials. The president of the university denied this, stating that he had not known of any CIA connection with the project, but Lyman Kirkpatrick, who during that period was executive director of the CIA, admitted that Michigan State had signed a contract with the CIA and had had full knowledge of the agency's role in the project.

Michigan State is only one of dozens of colleges, universities, and research centers which have had secret arrangements with the CIA. The Center for International Studies at the Massachusetts Institute of Technology was founded in 1951 under a secret CIA grant of money, and an assistant director of the CIA, Max F. Millikan, was made head of the Center. The connection with the CIA was revealed in 1964, and at that time officials at MIT implied that it was a thing of the past. However, fifteen percent of the Center's operating budget was still coming from the agency when, in 1966,

MIT announced that the Center had severed all connection with the CIA because of misunderstandings of its contracts with the organization.

Another strongly criticized link between the CIA and the academic world was revealed by *Ramparts* magazine in 1967. At that time the magazine described a long-secret arrangement between the agency and the National Students Association, which has chapters on more than three hundred American campuses. NSA leaders later admitted that the CIA had subsidized eighty percent of the association's annual budget for a period of fifteen years, had obtained draft deferments for NSA officers, and had paid the rent on the Washington headquarters of the student group. In all, it was estimated that $3 million was spent on the NSA—in return for which the CIA acquired NSA dossiers on foreign student leaders.

The methods used by the CIA with the student leaders were as much criticized as the operation itself. Each year the newly elected leaders of the association were approached and told that there were some secrets they should know about. Before being told the secrets, however, the students were asked to sign a security statement in which they promised not to divulge anything they were told. The penalty for violating the agreement was a twenty-year jail sentence under the National Security Act.

Then, as one student leader later put it, "they were told, 'You are employed by the CIA.' At that point they were trapped . . . a twenty-year jail sentence to maintain your integrity is a very high price to pay."

In defense of the CIA infiltration of the student group, Allen Dulles said, "If we turned back the Communists and made them milder and easier to live with, it was because we stopped them in certain areas, and the student area was one of them."

This Cold War concept dates back to the early nineteen fifties when the Soviet Union, operating through a variety of fronts, was attempting to infiltrate a great number of international organizations, including student groups. In its own defense, the CIA claims that it was only fighting fire with fire, and that the financing of the NSA had to be kept secret in order to give the student organization an appearance of independence. As Robert Amory, the former CIA deputy director for intelligence, said, "If we hadn't done this, we could have just been run over by the Commie front organizations."

The morality, not to mention the logic, of fighting fire with fire is, of course, open to question. Equally questionable is a secondary CIA defense for keeping the NSA subsidies secret. The CIA, claim its defenders, had to operate secretly because during the McCarthy era the American people would have objected strenuously to government subsidies to left-wing groups such as the NSA. However, the NSA is hardly a left-wing organization, and although some left-of-center groups have benefited from the CIA's domestic budget, reliable estimates indicate that only twenty percent of the agency's money goes to liberal causes abroad.

The public disclosure of the CIA connection with the National Students Association was an embarrassing pill for the CIA to swallow, for only seven months before,

Director Richard Helms had gone before the Senate Foreign Relations Committee and stated firmly that the CIA did not use the American student exchange program as a cover for espionage.

While the Central Intelligence Agency is responsible for espionage activities outside the United States, the Federal Bureau of Investigation is responsible for counterintelligence within the country. The FBI was established in 1907 as an investigating agency with federal powers operating under the direction of the Department of Justice. Its original purpose was to combat crime in the United States by overriding the conflicting police powers of the various states—a conflict which often left local police officials helpless. During World War I the bureau undertook certain security work in collaboration with the army and navy counterintelligence corps, and since then has grown into its present position as the primary counterintelligence organization in the country. During World War II the bureau marked up notable successes in capturing German spies who were landed from submarines on the East Coast, and also cracked a prewar German spy ring which had been transmitting information to Hamburg from a clandestine radio station on Long Island. During the Cold War period the FBI scored often in the war of wits it waged with Russian agents, its best-known cases being the capture of Rudolf Abel and the compilation of the evidence which led to the trial and execution of the Rosenbergs.

Since 1924 the director of the FBI has been J. Edgar Hoover, and since assuming control he has become one of the most powerful men in the United States and a virtual political untouchable. No American president has had the political courage to fire Hoover, although many have wished to do so, and Senator Eugene McCarthy, during his unsuccessful bid for the Democratic Party nomination in 1968, announced that if he were elected President he would definitely do it. Hoover has been in conflict with most of the modern administrations under which he has served, he is well past the mandatory retirement age for federal employees, and he could easily be removed by the attorney general, yet he remains, an influential and dedicated man whose very name produces controversy.

In many ways, Hoover *is* the FBI: his attitudes shape the thinking of every one of the fifteen thousand men and women in the bureau. His virulent brand of anti-Communism pervades the organization, as do his attitudes on dress and personal habits. The uniform for the FBI man until recently was a dark suit with padded shoulders, peaked lapels, and floppy trousers: the type of suit Hoover wore as a young man and still wears today. According to Norman Ollestad, a former FBI agent whose book, *Inside the FBI*, was a sharp attack on the organization, button-down shirts are frowned upon—only left-wing radicals wear them. Haircuts may not be too long or too short: long hair spells "intellectual" to the FBI, while short hair means "college boy," and both types are potential "radicals." Horse racing is in for

FBI men, but nightclubs are out: Hoover loves the horses. The mark of J. Edgar Hoover is on every member of his organization, but whatever one may think of that mark, it has produced a corps of disciplined and dedicated men.

Among Washingtonians, the FBI is known simply as "the Bureau," just as the CIA is known as "the Agency." The twin monoliths of security and intelligence cooperate with each other, as indeed they must, but generally in an air of bureaucratic mistrust. Although the functions of the two groups are intended to be separate, in practice they sometimes overlap with confusing results. An example is the infiltration of Cuban refugee groups in Miami by both the FBI and the CIA. Cuba is obviously the CIA's pigeon, while Miami belongs to the FBI, but both the agencies operate secretly within the multitude of factions and parties which have sprung up in the community of refugees from Castro's Cuba. Since these infiltrations are not coordinated, the FBI and the CIA often wind up competing with each other for the same information.

This duplication of effort is less the fault of the FBI than it is part of a general trend by the CIA to stray from the limitations originally set upon it by Congress. The National Security Act, which created the CIA, specifically stated that "the agency shall have no police, subpoena, law-enforcement powers, or internal security functions." Yet the agency is active on American campuses, scrambles for information in Miami, and has offices in most major cities across the country. As we have seen, however, the "blank check" clause in the CIA charter which allows it to "perform other functions and duties" is the loophole through which the CIA's role in national affairs has been broadened far beyond the intent of the lawmakers who created the agency.

So broad have these powers become that former President Harry S Truman, who sponsored the National Security Act, was moved to say in 1963, "I never had any thought . . . when I set up the CIA that it would be injected into peacetime cloak-and-dagger operations. . . . I would like to see the CIA be restored to its original assignment as the intelligence arm of the President. . . . There is something about the way the CIA has been functioning that is casting a shadow over our historic position and I feel we need to correct it."

The CIA's first step away from the purposes set forth in its charter came as early as 1948 when the National Security Council issued a secret paper, NSC 10/2, in which it authorized special CIA operations, provided that total secrecy was maintained and that the operations were small enough that the government could deny responsibility for them. The same paper created a bureau within the CIA for these operations under the title of the Office of Policy Coordination. Frank Wisner, a former OSS agent, was named to head the operations, and in 1951 the name of the section was changed to the Plans Division. That is the name it has held ever since, and the division has sole control over all secret operations. It was this division that ran the U-2 program, that directed the Bay of Pigs invasion, that successfully overthrew the left-wing governments in Iran and Guatemala. And it was the Plans Division which procured and published the speech by Nikita Khrushchev before the Twentieth Communist Party Congress in Moscow in which he secretly denounced Joseph Stalin.

The Plans Division also conducts many domestic operations supposedly prohibited by the National Security Act. Acting under permissive directives from the National Security Council, the Division interviews businessmen, students, and tourists before and after they visit Communist countries. The Division is also empowered to question persons within the United States, provided that prior permission is granted by the FBI. The Plans Division also supplies weapons to foreign countries for counter-insurgency operations, frequently through private companies.

The work of the Plans Division in Iran could stand as a classic example of espionage and subversion. The operation was mounted in collaboration with the British, with the American Embassy in Teheran as a base, and resulted in the overthrow of the government of Premier Mohammed Mossadegh. The premier had seized Britain's monopolistic oil holdings in Iran and was considered by the CIA to be under Soviet influence. The Plans Division stage-managed a series of riots and mob scenes in the streets of Teheran and topped off the operation with a full-fledged army revolt. Within forty-eight hours Mossadegh was in jail and a pro-American government was in power in Iran.

In planning and executing this coup there is little

doubt that the CIA violated its mandate by indulging in policy-making. By contrast, the Guatemala affair was a case of the CIA at its best. There the agency performed perfectly the function for which it was designed. Information was gathered, transmitted to headquarters, speedily evaluated, and passed on for the guidance of those in the executive branch of the government whose job it was to make policy. Unlike Iran, in Guatemala the CIA simply told its story to the National Security Council and from there the Defense Department took over.

By 1954 Guatemala had acquired the first Communist government in the Western hemisphere under the presidency of Jacobo Arbenz Guzman. Previously the economy of the country had been dominated by three large American corporations, the largest being the United Fruit Company, and the people had cried out for social reform. The reform came, but with it came fellow-traveling President Arbenz and a regime close to its borders which obviously could not be tolerated by the United States. The only local opposition to Arbenz came from Colonel Carlos Castillo Armas, who led a small army-in-exile in neighboring Honduras. The Hondurans sheltered Castillo's ragged army but they did so nervously, fearing that Arbenz might use their hospitality as a pretext for invasion. There was even talk that should Arbenz invade Honduras, then El Salvador too would fall and the thrust might reach the Panama Canal. All this, however, was in the realm of speculation, for it was well known that although Arbenz had the necessary troops to do the job, his army was woefully short of modern weapons. Thus the situation was one of delicate balance: Arbenz and Castillo each lacking sufficient arms to move against the other.

The weight which was to upset this delicate balance was the Swedish freighter *Alfhem*. Early in April 1954 she called at the Oder River port city of Stettin in Communist Poland to receive more than fifteen thousand crates of cargo in her hold. The cargo had arrived from Czechoslovakia the week before and consisted of munitions from the Skoda arms works. The rumors in Stettin were that the shipment was headed for someplace in the Western Hemisphere.

In Stettin at that time was a middle-aged German businessman who had come to Poland to negotiate for a machine tool factory. The weather was warm that April in Stettin and the German often took his lunch in a paper bag to eat on a hilltop that overlooked the dock area. He seemed to be something of a nature lover, for with him he always brought a pair of field glasses to observe the birds in the nearby trees. And sometimes his glasses would sweep along the piers to where the freighters, the *Alfhem* among them, were loading. After one particular bird-watching session he went back to his office and dictated a long letter to his secretary. The letter was addressed to a French manufacturing concern and was filled with impressive statistics, but the Frenchman who received it was interested less in statistics than in the period at the end of the second sentence. Under the period he found the microdot he had hoped would be there.

The microdot was turned over to a CIA technician in Paris who enlarged it and turned over the resultant code message to his resident radio operator. That night the decoded message was in Washington, and in the hands of Allen Dulles.

Never in peacetime have the movements of a ship been followed as carefully as were those of the *Alfhem*. CIA inquiries in Stockholm disclosed that she was supposed to be carrying a shipment of optical equipment to the French West African port of Dakar, but two days out of Dakar the *Alfhem* received orders to change course to the Honduras port of Trujillo. Then a CIA Caribbean agent reported that once again the course had been changed. Two days out of Trujillo, the *Alfhem* was told to proceed to the port of Puerto Barrios in Guatemala. Once in Puerto Barrios, a tight security cordon was placed around the ship, but the next day the CIA in Washington had the message: the fifteen thousand crates contained two thousand tons of small arms, small-arms ammunition, and light artillery pieces. It was enough to tip the balance: thus equipped, Arbenz could take both Honduras and El Salvador and dominate Central America.

The CIA had now performed two of the three main functions of an intelligence organization. It had found the information and had transmitted it speedily. The third function was to evaluate the intelligence, and with the information in hand Dulles called an emergency meeting of the Intelligence Advisory Committee, the forerunner of the U. S. Intelligence Board. The conferees quickly agreed on an evaluation of the intelligence: Arbenz was planning aggressive war. The next day Dulles presented the evaluation to the National Security Council. Although his paper did not make specific recommendations it pointed out the dangers involved and reminded the Council of the existence of Castillo's poorly armed band in the jungles of Honduras. This was intelligence work at its finest: clear and accurate, and with no attempt to influence policy.

One week later the Department of Defense, not the CIA, dispatched two huge Air Force Globemasters to Honduras and Nicaragua. Each of the cargo planes carried more than twenty-five tons of munitions. When the arms had been distributed, each of Colonel Castillo's men was equipped with a light submachine gun, a pistol, and a machete. At the same time, three obsolete Air Force B-26 bombers happened to find their way into Castillo's hands. The balance had been tipped the other way.

The clash between the forces of Arbenz and Castillo was almost anticlimactic to the intelligence battle which preceded it. The three P-38 fighters which constituted the Guatemalan Air Force were so intimidated by the larger bombers that they defected at once to the other side. Castillo crossed the border and issued an ultimatum calling on Arbenz to surrender. The Guatemalan Army, deciding that Communism was a dead horse in Guatemala and that Castillo looked like a winner, went on strike, Arbenz fled the country, and Castillo took over as the head of an anti-Communist junta.

Guatemala was a case of good intelligence used

wisely. Nothing is more frustrating to the agent in the field than to see intelligence, which he has carefully gathered and transmitted, either disregarded or evaluated improperly. General Doolittle, speaking to the Senate Committee on Armed Services, said in 1957: "The acquisition of intelligence is one thing, the interpretation of intelligence is another, and the use of that intelligence is a third." In Guatemala, the CIA did all three well.

The same cannot be said of the CIA's Cuban adventure, which has been called one of the most poorly planned and executed military operations in history. Of it, Lyman B. Kirkpatrick, Jr., once the executive director of the CIA, has said: "One of the most painful episodes of my entire career in intelligence, both personally and officially, was the ill-fated operation to liberate Cuba from Communism, now known throughout the world as the Bay of Pigs."

Even today, all the reasons for the disaster are not yet clear. When it was all over, President Kennedy, in a natural desire to avoid naming any one scapegoat, remarked unhappily, "There's enough blame to go around." And indeed there was. The President's own staff and his military advisers in the Pentagon performed in something less than brilliant fashion, but the primary blame must go to the CIA. The Cuban invasion was a CIA creation from beginning to end, and it failed because of two characteristics which seem to mark every operation of the agency. The first is the CIA's refusal to believe in any intelligence but its own; the second is the agency's traditional unwillingness to deal with any local group that is not on the far right of the political spectrum.

In its own defense, the CIA feels that as one of the two largest information-gathering services in the world it has the right to believe in its own infallibility. Their attitude seems to be, "After all, who could know more than we do?" As for supporting right-wing groups, Allen Dulles said more than once, "We support our friends. Do you suggest that we support our enemies?"

The first argument is irrational and the second is simplistic. No agency can possibly know *every* fact about a given situation, and the peoples of the world are simply *not* divided into good guys and bad guys.

The information that the CIA gathered before the Cuban invasion was good—in a sense it was too good to justify what came later. After the affair was over the State Department issued a report in which it stated that the Soviet Union had poured more than thirty thousand tons of arms into Cuba in the previous year. In addition, the State Department knew that the Cuban defenders were armed with "Soviet JS-2 51-ton tanks, Soviet SU-100 assault guns, Soviet T-34 35-ton tanks, Soviet 76-mm field guns, Soviet 85-mm field guns, Soviet 122-mm field guns. . . ." The report also stated that Fidel Castro's Cuba had the largest ground forces in Latin America, 250,000 regular soldiers and 150,000 militia, noting that on the basis of the regular army alone, "one out of every thirty Cubans is today in the armed forces, as against one in fifty in the Soviet Union and one in sixty in the United States."

All this the CIA knew, and against this array of power the agency decided to mount an invasion with a force of 1400 men.

Defending their decision, CIA officials explained that an essential part of the strategy was for the invading force to strike for the safety of the Escambray Mountains. Once in this mountain stronghold, they claimed, the invaders could entrench themselves—as Castro himself had done years before—while hundreds of thousands of Cubans flocked to the cause. The CIA people were firm about this. They knew it would happen. Their intelligence reports told them that it would.

In the light of what finally happened, we have no way of knowing whether such support from the Cuban people would have been forthcoming. But such a plan would have needed the active support of the one organization within Cuba with a broad popular appeal and with an effective anti-Castro underground. This was the anti-Castro People's Revolutionary Movement (MRP) headed by Manolo Antonio Ray. The MRP was a model of underground organization with a network that covered the island, executive councils in every province, and a chain of command that reached to the most remote villages. No small force of insurgents invading Cuba could hope to succeed without the help of the MRP, and the MRP was ready to work with any group that would overthrow Castro. But Allen Dulles and his aides decided that the moderately liberal MRP was too left-wing to be trusted, and preference went instead to the Movement for Revolutionary Recovery (MRR)—a right-wing outfit composed of former military officers, business and professional men, and castoffs from the days of dictator Fulgencio Batista.

Manolo Ray was a former minister in Castro's cabinet who had broken with Fidel on the question of Communism. When it became clear that Castro's flirtation with Marxism had turned into a torrid love affair, Ray went underground and began to form his organization. He stayed in Cuba for eight months, constantly on the run, until he was satisfied that his network was operating efficiently. Then he left Cuba by sea one night and turned up the following week in Florida, ready to work with anyone who would help to depose Castro. But to the CIA, Manolo Ray was a political leper. He favored continuing Castro's land reform program, and he advocated a mixed economy of private enterprise, government ownership of utilities, and the nationalization of certain industries. This was far too radical for the CIA, and in the refugee centers in Miami the word was passed that Ray was untouchable. Ray soon became the target of reactionary Cuban businessmen and politicians, and his influence was severely limited.

Getting the various Cuban exile factions to cooperate in a united front was a difficult but necessary task for the CIA. The Revolutionary Democratic Front was eventually formed, and although it embraced all the groups operating in Miami, including Ray's MRP, the conservative MRR was given the position of dominance. Several farms in the backwater country of Florida were leased as training camps for the newly formed Liberation Army, and financial backing was obtained from various American corporations with interests in Cuba. To head the operation, Dulles named his top deputy, Richard M. Bissell, a former Yale economics instructor. Bissell decided that training a foreign army on American soil was too compromising a position to be risked, and arrangements were made with the pro-American government in Guatemala for a training camp to be made available to the Liberation Army. The site chosen was far back in the jungle on acreage belonging to a wealthy Guatemalan named Robert Alejos, and soon airstrips had been built and CIA pilots in mufti were ferrying in men and supplies.

When President Kennedy entered office in January 1961, he inherited the plans for the Cuban invasion from his predecessor, President Eisenhower. By that time the timetable was well advanced: the troops were in training in Guatemala, and the Bay of Pigs had been chosen as the invasion beachhead. Lacking any personal knowledge of the situation, the new President was forced to rely on the estimates prepared by his White House aides and Pentagon advisers. These aides, in turn, relied on the CIA evaluation of the situation, which, as we have seen, was overly optimistic. Short of calling a halt to the whole operation, there was little that Kennedy could do to alter events, but he did issue an order excluding any supporters of former Cuban dictator Batista from the Liberation Army. These *Batistianos*, most of them thugs and former secret policemen, were the most hated men in Cuba, and their presence in the Liberation Army would do nothing to endear the invaders to the hearts of the Cuban people. In a striking example of how the intelligence tail can wag the political dog, the CIA refused to put the President's order into effect. From the CIA point of view, the *Batistianos* were experienced military men with, of course, the desirable right-wing tinge to their politics. The fact that they were torturers and murderers despised by the Cuban people was considered secondary. The CIA was fighting fire with fire again.

Kennedy was unaware until after the invasion that his ban on the *Batistianos* had been ignored. Nor did he know until too late that Manolo Ray and the MRP had been refused the financial aid and weapons which had been given to other anti-Castro groups. He did not know that the MRP members of the Liberation Army had been systematically excluded from positions of command, and that when two hundred of the soldiers objected to serving under a *Batistiano* officer they were arrested and isolated under guard from the rest of the troops. He did not know that one hundred and twenty MRP members en route to the training camps in Guatemala had been detained in Florida by CIA agents and would never take part in the invasion. And he did not know that the choice for commander of the expedition, Manuel Artime Buesa, was a twenty-nine-year-old soldier of limited experience. All Kennedy knew was what Dulles and Bissell told him: that the troops were raring to go, that there would be uprisings in Cuba supporting the invasion, that the beachhead could be held, and that the rebels would be able to establish a government on Cuban soil which the United States could then recognize. Actually, what the President did or did not know was relatively unimportant;

the operation was much too far advanced for changes to be made.

The military plans for the invasion of Cuba called for two air strikes by insurgent Cuban bombers on Castro's airfields, followed by a paratroop drop inland from the beachhead, and then by the main seaborne assault at the Bay of Pigs by five battalions of the Liberation Army. The operation was to be wholly a Cuban one; no American forces were to take part or to acknowledge any connection with the invading troops. The Cuban leaders wanted it that way. There were no doubts in their minds, or the CIA's, that once the beachhead was established their countrymen would come to their aid. There was never any question about American participation in a *successful* invasion, but once the Cuban affair was over it became clear that the Liberation Army leaders had expected American aid should the invasion appear to falter or fail. The Americans who took part in the operation, both CIA and army personnel, have always maintained that no such commitment was ever made. Not surprisingly, these conflicting accounts have led to bitterness on both sides. Considering the two points of view, Lyman B. Kirkpatrick, Jr., concluded: "I am quite convinced that the truth lies somewhere in between. It seems most likely that while the Americans didn't go so far as to say that United States forces would actually land in Cuba, it is only fair to suspect that in the excitement and emotional heat just before the landing they must certainly have been as encouraging as possible."

The first air strike by Cuban-piloted B-26 bombers

took place on April 15 and was considered a success. Post-strike photographs and reports from pilots indicated that most of Castro's Air Force had been destroyed on the ground and the Cuban leaders were jubilant. The CIA at once informed President Kennedy that the Cuban Air Force had been rendered ineffective. This was not quite so.

In the early hours of April 16 the five battalions of the Liberation Army went ashore at the Bay of Pigs, debarking from five Liberty ships which had been chartered by the CIA under dummy names. At the same time C-54 and C-46 transport planes based in Guatemala and Nicaragua arrived over the beachhead and dropped their paratroopers inland. Air cover was provided by eight of the old B-26 bombers, reinforced by several obsolete P-51 fighters. The battle was joined.

But thousands of miles away at the United Nations in New York another battle was taking place, a battle of words. In this arena of world opinion the United States was at once attacked by the Communist countries for aiding and provoking the invasion of Cuba. The American ambassador to the United Nations, Adlai Stevenson, delivered an impassioned defense of his country in which he denied any American association with the Liberation Army. His speech sounded most effective, for he truly believed what he was saying; Kennedy had kept him in the dark on all phases of the Cuban operation. Stevenson learned later in the day that he had been deceived and that his credibility had been dangerously weakened. He was furious, and in a heated conversation with the President he insisted that there be no more air strikes. Secretary of State Dean Rusk supported this position. Because of this opposition within his own cabinet, and because the CIA had assured him that the Cuban Air Force had been crippled, Kennedy canceled the second air strike.

The Cuban Air Force had been damaged, but not destroyed. Five jet aircraft were still operable: three American-made T-33 trainers and two British Sea Furies. The next morning the five jets appeared over the beachhead and turned the balance of battle. With no opposition from the air the jets sank two of the Liberty ships —the two vital ones carrying ammunition and communications equipment—and chased the others out to sea. The invasion had been effectively defeated but the Liberation Army fought on, inflicting heavy losses on the Castro forces which soon surrounded them. There was no doubt about the courage and ability of the invading troops, but with Castro's jets controlling the air the Liberation Army could not be resupplied or reinforced. On the second day the Soviet tanks and heavy guns arrived at the battle area, traveling over roads which could have been cut by Manolo Ray's underground, had they been given the order. By the third day it was all over: the Liberation Army surrendered.

Why did the operation fail? The question was asked across the nation in high places and low in an orgy of self-recrimination. Commissions were appointed inside and outside the government to examine the role of the CIA in the affair. These commissions could study only the operational mistakes, and these alone were damning. One high CIA official admitted that the operation had not succeeded "because there had been a complete miscalculation by the CIA operators of what was required to do the job. If there had even been a moment during the battle when the Brigade [i.e., the Liberation Army] had been near to achieving victory, then we might be able to say that it had been close. In my opinion, the outcome was never close and even to this day there is serious question whether it would have succeeded even if the H-hour air strike had been permitted, *and even if Castro had no airplanes or tanks to put into the battle*" (authors' italics).

But aside from a review of operational mistakes, there was another lesson to be learned from the Bay of Pigs disaster. More important than air cover or armament or logistical support was the question of the role of the CIA in making and influencing national policy. Over the years, as various aspects of the operation have been made public, it has become clear that the invasion of Cuba was virtually a private enterprise conducted by a small group of men divorced from the control of their government. The creation of the President's Foreign Intelligence Board and the limitation of the CIA's operational powers indicate that the lesson was learned, but we do not know for how long. To students of espionage the Bay of Pigs taught another lesson: it is rarely possible for a large nation such as the United States to accomplish something by irregular means which it is not prepared to accomplish by diplomacy or direct military action. Espionage is a means, but it is never an end in itself.

9 FROM THE EARTH TO THE STARS

Not all CIA operations involve invasion and subversion, plots and counterplots. The great bulk of CIA employees perform jobs which in private industry would be considered routine. These "white" employees work under their own names as scientists, engineers, economists, translators, and many other mundane occupations. A white CIA employee may simply be a reader, although a specialized one. Eighty percent of all the information obtained from Communist countries comes from open sources such as books, newspapers, and magazines. The CIA buys every possible Communist publication; 200,000 pieces of literature are delivered to Langley every month. No publication is too prosaic when placed in the hands of an expert reader who can find significance in the changes on a road map or the alteration of a railroad timetable. In one case the plans for the mechanization of the Czech Army were uncovered by an agent whose quest began when he saw the name of a Russian expert in tank warfare mentioned in a local Czech newspaper.

These white operators are the backbone of an espionage system, but such activities rarely come to the public eye. The publicized side of espionage, the coups and exploits of "black" operators, are what attract our attention, and they conceal the routine work of white operators behind a curtain of glamour and romance. These exploits range from the earth to the stars, and are the stuff from which thrillers are made. In truth, they are more thrilling than the fiction which apes them.

One of the CIA's most famous coups was the Berlin tunnel in the mid-1950's, which won the agency the admiration of the Russians themselves. Just outside West Berlin in the East Zone of Germany, CIA agents discovered a terminus of telephone cables serving both East German and Soviet military headquarters, and civilian officials as well. The telephone junction was a mass of wiring which could handle over four hundred calls simultaneously, and when news of the find came to Langley, the plotters in the Plans Division went to work.

Given modern techniques, the operation was not a difficult one, but precision was necessary. On the Western side of the border American military authorities began to erect a building whose purpose was shrouded in secrecy. But after a week or two there were the usual security leaks and soon everyone in that neighborhood of West Berlin knew that the Americans were building an experimental radar station. By the time the building was finished it was part of the landscape and taken for granted. The building, of course, was a hollow shell and served only as a base for a major tunneling operation. The tunnel was dug from the basement of the so-called radar station and was aimed precisely at the telephone terminus which was located six hundred yards away, five feet under the village of Alt-Glienicke in East Germany.

Every secret tunneling job has one major problem: where do you put the dirt? Inside the radar building CIA agents packed hundreds of tons of loam and clay into wooden packing crates labeled as radar equipment. The boxes were shipped out in daylight under the noses of the curious, and new boxes shipped in daily. This went on for months. The tunnel took that long because of the secrecy involved, but when it was finished it was a tribute to American engineering skill. The tunnel itself was framed with corrugated iron, and was complete with drainage pipes and air conditioning. More important, it ended within striking distance of the telephone junction.

The next step was to tap the terminus, and this too was done in style. Tapping wires protected by thick layers of lead were run through a wooden partition at the tunnel's end, then through two steel doors and into the terminus. Expert technicians flown in for the job attached the taps to the telephone cables so adroitly that service was not interrupted for a second. Then the tapping wires were connected to over four hundred amplifying units back in the deluxe tunnel. The amplifiers boosted the impulses on the long-distance lines, then relayed them through a distributor unit to the "radar" station where over four hundred tape recorders, one for each line, were ready to record Red messages. Then, borrowing a page from the OSS, the CIA agents placed a sign on the East German side of the steel door which covered the tapping wires. In Russian, it read, "No admittance by order of the commanding officer."

If the tunnel had lasted a month it would have been considered a success, and worth the money and effort expended. In fact, it lasted almost a year, and during that time the CIA recorded hundreds of thousands of messages between Soviet and East German military commanders. Millions of words were recorded on tape and shipped to Langley where scores of white employees analyzed the messages and prepared evaluations for the proper authorities. It was an operation of unprecedented value.

The taps were finally discovered by a squad of Russian signal troops making a routine check of the terminus. One young soldier spotted a stray wire which simply did not belong where it was. The impressive sign on the steel door prevented him from tracing the wire, but he decided to apply for permission from above. After some confusion the permission was granted and Russian troops broke down the door. By then, however, an alarm had been sounded back in the radar station, triggered by a device the moment the first soldier touched the tapping wire. By the time the Soviet troops broke through, the tunnel had been cleared and blocked on the American end.

Moscow sent an indignant note to Washington demanding punishment of those who had perpetrated "subterranean espionage." But at the same time the Russian and the East German press referred to the incident as a "bold, skillful, and daring operation." So impressed were the Russians that they eventually opened the tunnel as a tourist attraction, with guides to explain the intricacies of wiretapping to the curious. Across the barriers that separate East and West, it was the tip of the hat from one clever professional opponent to another.

From the earth below East Germany to the stars above Soviet Sverdlovsk; from an air-conditioned tunnel to a ghostlike aircraft flying seventeen miles above the earth's surface; from a tapped telephone line to the most sophisticated recording devices etching photographs and radar signals on miles of whirring tapes; from the Berlin tunnel to Francis Gary Powers and the U-2. And beyond to the naval ship U.S.S. *Pueblo*, off the coast of North Korea in February of 1968.

Despite the political repercussions which occurred when Powers and his U-2 were shot down over Russia, the air reconnaissance program as a whole remains as the greatest triumph achieved by the CIA. It was intelligence work on a mass production basis, never to be equaled by conventional means. Today its achievements are rivaled only by the spy-in-the-sky satellites whirling far higher over the earth than any aircraft can venture. But satellites are cold, impersonal things; men sat in the cockpits of the U-2 planes and risked their lives in the most dangerous of espionage games.

The story of the U-2 begins in 1953 at the Lockheed Aircraft Corporation in Burbank, California. At that time the F-104 fighter possessed the greatest range and highest altitude capability of any operational aircraft in the United States. Lockheed engineers were instructed to design a plane that would outstrip the F-104, something that could range as high as ninety thousand feet, stay aloft for eight hours, and cover up to four thousand miles. The result was the U-2, a plane that was practically a glider with a jet engine attached, for in order to cover those tremendous distances the aircraft would have to half-fly, half-glide, in an enormous arc above the earth's surface. The pilot, too, would have to be a man of combined talents: part conventional flyer, and part astronaut encased in a spacesuit, his helmet sealed to his body by a cork ring. The U-2 met the specifications required; it was an impressive aeronautical achievement.

The U-2 was first used by the Air Force for high-altitude scientific research, measuring radioactive fallout and atmospheric turbulence. The National Aeronautics and Space Administration also used the craft to observe missiles in flight and to track the paths of nose cones on the way down. Then the CIA became interested in the U-2, for it was obviously the best plane ever designed for spying. By 1956 the CIA had organized a group of eight civilian pilots, including Francis Gary Powers, who arrived at Incirlik Air Base in Turkey with their wives and families. The CIA group was promptly isolated from the rest of the base in a trailer camp where they lived in seclusion for nearly four years. Those four years were the heyday of the U-2.

During those years the 10-10 Reconnaissance Detachment, as the group was called, flew a series of long-distance missions over the Soviet Union with virtual immunity. The U-2 could fly higher and farther than any interceptor aircraft, and at that time there was no missile built that could come close to catching the elusive ghost plane. Each of the U-2s was loaded with equipment for the mechanical and electronic collection of intelligence. From fifteen miles above the earth the U-2 cameras could take pictures clear enough to enable viewers to count the stripes on a football field and distinguish between a man on a bicycle and a man on a motorbike. During those four years the U-2 flights located Soviet missile stations, atomic testing grounds, airfields, troop concentrations, and were even able to record the design of various Russian railway bridges. Other equipment aboard the U-2s located Soviet radar stations and, by recording the signals given out by those stations, enabled CIA experts to expose whole areas of the Russian antiaircraft defense system. And while all this was going on the Russians could only fume impotently. They knew of the intrusions over their territory; their radar stations recorded every overflight. But they were helpless to stop the U-2 missions, and rather than admit this helplessness to the world they kept quiet, and waited.

For the record, the men of the 10-10 Reconnaissance Detachment were employed by the Lockheed Aircraft

Corporation, and were on loan to the National Advisory Committee for Aeronautics. In actuality, the pilots were under contract to the CIA, and were paid a monthly salary of $2500. The pay was high, but the pilots earned it. In addition to the flying hazards involved, each pilot was often in the air for eight hours, sealed inside a spacesuit and unable to eat or drink. Before each flight the pilots had to spend an hour and a half inside the suit breathing pure oxygen, and they often landed in a state of physical exhaustion, bodies bruised from the tight-fitting suits and throats parched with thirst.

In April 1960 the 10-10 Detachment was transferred from Turkey to the U. S. Air Force Base at Peshawar, Pakistan. The reason for this move has never been made public, but it seems apparent that after four years the flights out of Turkey had served their purpose, and that a new section of the Soviet Union was about to be exposed to the U-2's merciless eye. After four days at Peshawar, Francis Gary Powers was chosen to make the first flight from the new base. What the men of the 10-10 Detachment did not know, however, was that the mission would also inaugurate a new era in reconnaissance flying. The Russians had perfected the SA-2 missile, and the U-2 was no longer invulnerable.

On the morning of May 1, 1960, Powers sat in his aircraft, studying the map which was strapped to his thigh while he waited for permission to take off. The course he was to take was plotted in red and blue pencils, and covered thirty-three hundred miles from Peshawar across the Soviet Union to Bodo Airport in Norway. It would take him over the Aral Sea, Sverdlovsk, Kirov,

Archangel, and Murmansk before he began the long, gliding descent to Bodo. He considered the mission routine; he had made many similar flights before.

As he waited at the end of the Peshawar runway, Francis Gary Powers was probably the most gaudily equipped spy ever about to set forth on an espionage mission. In addition to his billion-dollar aircraft and the millions of dollars of equipment it contained, Powers carried a silenced revolver, two hundred rounds of ammunition, a dagger, fishing gear, a pneumatic boat, detailed maps of the Soviet Union, chemical aids for making campfires, signal flares, compasses, a handsaw, an electric flashlight, food concentrates, 7500 rubles in Soviet currency, a package of gold coins, and an assortment of rings and wristwatches to be used to bribe people should he be forced down. Less optimistically, he also had a hollow American silver dollar filled with poison and fitted with a pin. In the same vein of macabre preparation, the aircraft was fitted with an explosive device which the pilot could use should he choose not to fall into Russian hands. Powers was ready for every contingency.

Taking off from Peshawar, Powers quickly brought his U-2 to a cruising altitude of sixty thousand feet, clearing the mountain peaks that mark the border of Afghanistan, and crossing into the Soviet Union. As he crossed the border he pushed five special controls which activated his intelligence-gathering machinery. Then he settled back for the flight.

But back across the border the American radio operators monitoring the Russian control system realized that the flight would be anything but routine. As Powers intruded into Soviet airspace the monitors noted that the U-2 had been picked up by Russian radar almost at once. This, in itself, was not unusual, but the monitors could also hear the conversations of Soviet pilots, and it soon became clear that a relay of supersonic fighters had been sent up to shoot Powers down. This had never happened before; the Russians *knew* that their interceptors could not fly high enough to reach the U-2. Then they heard from the pilot himself. Just above Sverdlovsk, Powers radioed to report a flame-out in his jet engine. He said that he would descend to forty thousand feet and try to start the engine again. That was the last report he made.

There has been some dispute as to exactly how Powers was shot down, and the question has been further confused by the presence of Soviet fighters in the vicinity. We now know that the fighters were there not to fire on Powers but to help in tracking the course of the U-2. Once the course was established, fourteen SA-2 missiles were fired. Powers saw an orange flash, and then his aircraft went into a dive. During the long descent he lost consciousness several times and was pressed against the controls, unable to use the catapulting device to bail out. He finally managed to raise the canopy and get out through the top; his parachute then opened automatically.

The Russian report said simply that the U-2 was shot down by a rocket at 8:53 A.M. The Russians made no mention of a subsequent report that one of the fourteen rockets fired hit a MIG-19 of the group that was trailing Powers, destroying the plane and killing the pilot. Oleg Penkovskiy mentions the incident in his memoirs, and Powers himself later said that when he reached the ground and was surrounded by Russian farm workers, one of them raised two fingers, as if to ask if there were two pilots. "I told him no," Powers said, "just shook my head no, and pointed to myself and held up one finger, telling him that I was alone. Then he pointed up in the air and I looked up and saw what I think was a parachute, but I knew that I had no other parachute aboard the aircraft."

The SA-2 missile that knocked Francis Gary Powers out of the sky also ended the U-2 reconnaissance program. For five days after Powers was downed, no one but the Russians knew that he was still alive. While KGB officials were interrogating the pilot at Lubianka headquarters, the CIA put out a cover story saying that a single-engine U. S. Air Force plane engaged on a weather reconnaissance mission was missing in the mountains between the Soviet Union and Turkey. This story had been prepared well in advance, and it might have worked had Powers been killed in the crash. But Powers was alive, and talking. This was in accordance with CIA instructions: if captured, tell everything and try and save yourself, for there is little that your captors will not know, anyway. Then, after five days of silence, Nikita Khrushchev announced that an American spy plane had been shot down over the Soviet Union—he made no mention of the pilot. Still hoping that Powers was dead, American officials continued to insist that the U-2 was a weather research plane, and that the Russians were trying to manufacture an international incident. But the next day, Khrushchev played his ace: he announced that the pilot was alive and had confessed to being a spy. President Eisenhower then took the unprecedented step of assuming full responsibility for the U-2 flight and admitting the act of espionage. He later announced that there would be no further U-2 flights over Soviet territory.

The political repercussions were severe. Khrushchev canceled an impending summit conference, explaining that he could not expect his countrymen to give President Eisenhower a cordial welcome after the U-2 affair. Domestic reaction was mixed, but on the whole the President was subjected to considerable criticism, not so much for authorizing the flights as for admitting it publicly. But, as his press secretary put it, it is a little difficult to disown a spy who has a U-2 strapped to his back. The same press secretary gave what was perhaps the most pointed moral to the story when he was asked by a reporter what lessons had been learned from the U-2 incident.

"Don't get caught," was his reply.

The reply, had Commander Lloyd M. Bucher of the U.S. Navy ship *Pueblo* heeded it five years later, might have saved him and his crew from a Communist prison. Cruising in North Korean waters in early February of 1968, the *Pueblo* ventured either too close to, or actually penetrated, the twelve-mile limit of international waters —the exact truth will probably never be known—and was promptly approached and seized by torpedo boats of the

North Korean Navy. When her officers and crew were imprisoned, a great cry rose up throughout America and in the Western press to set them free. There was talk of "piracy and hijacking on the high seas," and "acts of war." There was talk of retaliation. There was relatively little talk, however, about the unvarnished truth: crammed to her gunwales with an estimated $100 million worth of electronic devices which enabled her to listen in on Communist tactical communications, the U.S.S. *Pueblo* was a spy ship, and she had made the one irrevocable mistake of getting caught.

The *Pueblo* is evidence of the continuing revolution in modern espionage. In recent years the U-2 has been joined by drone aircraft and by orbiting spy-in-the-sky satellites such as the American Samos and Soviet Cosmos, which in their whirling flights around the earth snap highly detailed photographs of transportation systems, missile sites, troop concentrations, and nuclear installations. The dividends can be enormous—in 1964, photographs of Red China's nuclear test facilities at Lop Nor enabled the United States to predict the timing of Peking's first atomic explosion.

One of the best listening posts, however, is a naval vessel. Ships can carry far more electronic gear than satellites or jet airplanes; they can move about freely in international waters; and they can remain on patrol, "ears" finely attuned, for months on end. It is no secret that Russia's vast fleet of fishing trawlers—the largest in the world—includes at least twenty ships that carry more spying equipment than fishing tackle. These ships openly monitor American military activities from the U.S. base on Guam in the Pacific to the Polaris submarine base at Holy Loch, Scotland. The United States, on the other hand, disdains such obvious subterfuge and maintains three so-called "ferret" ships of the *Pueblo* type, as well as five converted merchantmen such as the U.S.S. *Liberty*, which was accidentally strafed by Israeli jets during the Six-Day War in 1967 when she ventured too close to the shores of Sinai in an attempt to record battle-field communications.

But even the data recorded by the Samos and Cosmos, two hundred miles above the earth's surface, must be interpreted finally by men. The U-2 and the *Pueblo*, sophisticated though they may be, are no more effective than the hands and intelligence of the men at their controls. The true spy, in the end, is a human being, a man, superbly equipped technologically and perhaps a product of twentieth-century materialism; but still—a man.

Francis Gary Powers, the captured U-2 pilot, was tried before a court in Moscow and sentenced to ten years imprisonment. Twenty months later he stood on the fog-shrouded bridge between East and West Berlin facing a bespectacled, gray-faced colonel of the KGB. As officials on both sides exchanged formalities, Francis Powers and Rudolf Abel stared at each other and waited for the ceremonies to end. They were both spies, but their lives could not have been more different. One was a young technician who spied from the stars, the other a weary old master of earthy espionage. But at that moment their differences seemed unimportant. They each had but one thought in mind: they were going home.

GLOSSARY
NOTES
BIBLIOGRAPHY
INDEX

GLOSSARY OF INTELLIGENCE JARGON

Terms change with the times, particularly in the field of intelligence where jargon was originally used to conceal the real meaning of the word. Some terms, however, seem to persist through the years, particularly in the Russian secret service. These are a few of them.

Apparat—   a group, an organization. In intelligence work, a spy ring. See *rezidentura*.

Black operator—   an agent working covertly or under cover, as opposed to a white operator (q.v.), who works openly.

C—   the initial traditionally used for the head of the British Secret Service, MI6.

Center—   Moscow headquarters, used by both KGB and GRU agents in the field.

Control—   in British parlance, the equivalent of a Russian *rezident* (q.v.), but sometimes used for higher, administrative officials.

The Corporation—   used by the KGB and the GRU for the local Communist Party in any particular country.

Cut-out—   an agent used as an intermediary as a security measure. Thus, Jones passes papers to Smith, who gives them to Brown. Smith is the cut-out, and Jones and Brown need never meet or even know each other's names.

Dead-drop—   a place where material can be left safely by one agent to be picked up by another. Radiator pipes and telephone booths are often used. Like the cut-out, the dead-drop avoids contact between agents.

Dubok—   Russian for a hollow oak tree; thus, a hiding place for secret documents.

Gammas—   one-time signal pads used for enciphering messages.

Illness—   arrest; to be taken ill is to be arrested, or to have one's cover broken. Similar terms: to get dirty, or bloody.

Infirmary or hospital—prison, from the above.

Istochnik—   the source of information; the agent who must first be recruited.

Korrektirovchik—   the agent who recruits the *istochnik* (q.v.).

Music box—   radio transmitter.

Nash—   a fellow Russian agent. Literally, "one of ours."

Neighbors—   see *sosedi*.

Novator—   the planner, the one in charge.

Parol—   a password and reply for recognition between agents. Often nonsensical to avoid mistaken identity. Thus, the parol might be, "Didn't I meet you in Miami at the races?" And the reply, "No, not me. I never go skiing."

Rezident—   the agent in the field in charge of operations against the target country.

Rezidentura—   the group of agents working under the *rezident*: a spy ring.

Roof—   used by Russians to designate a Communist front organization which can be used for cover.

Shoe—   a forged passport; thus, the man who manufactures false passports is the shoemaker.

Sosedi—   literally, "the neighbors." Used by GRU people when referring to the KGB. The KGB, in turn, refers to the GRU as "our military neighbors."

Tainik—   Russian for dead-drop (q.v.).

Treff—   a secret meeting.

White operator—   an agent who works openly without concealing his identity, as opposed to a black operator (q.v.).

Yafka—   a safe place for a meeting; a safe house.

GLOSSARY
OF ABBREVIATIONS

AEC—Atomic Energy Commission (U.S.).

Cheka—Extraordinary Commission for the Struggle Against Counter-Revolution and Sabotage (USSR).

CIA—Central Intelligence Agency (U.S.).

DCI—Director of Central Intelligence (Head of CIA).

DIA—Defense Intelligence Agency (U.S.).

DMI—Director of Military Intelligence (Great Britain).

FBI—Federal Bureau of Investigation (U.S.).

G-2—Army Intelligence (Staff designation) (U.S.).

GPU—State Political Directorate—Successor to Cheka, founded 1922 (USSR).

GRU—Chief Intelligence Directorate of the Ministry of Defense (Red Army Intelligence).

KGB—Committee of State Security. The combined espionage and counterespionage organization of the USSR.

KI—Information Committee set up to coordinate the activities of the KGB and the GRU. Since disbanded (USSR).

MGB—Ministry of State Security. Successor to the NKGB when all commissariats were renamed ministries (USSR).

MI5—Popular name for the Directorate General of Security Service (British counterintelligence).

MI6—Popular name for the Secret Service or Secret Intelligence Service (British intelligence).

NKGB—People's Commissariat of State Security. Subdepartment of the NKVD, which was elevated to a separate commissariat on two occasions, 1941 and 1943 (USSR).

NKVD—People's Commissariat of Internal Affairs. Total security organization which absorbed the OGPU in 1934 (USSR).

NSA—National Security Agency (U.S.).

NSC—National Security Council (U.S.).

OGPU—United State Political Directorate; successor to GPU, founded 1924 (USSR).

ONI—Office of Naval Intelligence (U.S.).

OSS—Office of Strategic Services (U.S.).

SMERSH—During World War II, a Russian military counterintelligence force with powers of summary execution.

SO, E—Special Operations, Executive (Great Britain).

NOTES

Many of the quotations in this work are from contemporary sources such as newspaper accounts and trial records. Some are from books listed in the Selected Bibliography whose authors are identified in the text. Sources for other book quotations are listed below.

Page 42—*The FBI's Most Famous Cases* by Andrew Tully.

Page 50—*Unmasked!* by Ronald Seth.

Page 52—*Spies of the Twentieth Century* by Charles Franklin.

Page 87—*School for Spies* by J. Bernard Hutton.

Pages 137–140 and 141–142—*Spy Ring* by John Bulloch and Henry Miller.

Pages 158 (student's speech), 163—*The Espionage Establishment* by David Wise and Thomas B. Ross.

Pages 175, 178—*The Real CIA* by Lyman B. Kirkpatrick, Jr.

A SELECTED BIBLIOGRAPHY

ALSOP, STEWART, and THOMAS BRADEN. *Sub Rosa: The OSS and American Espionage*. New York: Harcourt, 1946.

BULLOCH, JOHN, and HENRY MILLER. *Spy Ring*. London: Secker and Warburg, 1961.

CATER, DOUGLASS. *The Fourth Branch of Government*. Boston: Houghton Mifflin, 1959.

CHAMBERS, WHITTAKER. *Witness*. New York: Random, 1952.

COOKE, ALISTAIR. *A Generation on Trial*. New York: Knopf, 1950.

COOKRIDGE, E. H. *The Third Man*. New York: Putnam, 1968.

DERIABIN, PETER, and FRANK GIBNEY. *The Secret World*. New York: Doubleday, 1959.

DULLES, ALLEN. *The Craft of Intelligence*. New York: Harper, 1963.

———— (ed.). *Great True Spy Stories*. New York: Harper, 1968.

FOOTE, ALEXANDER. *Handbook for Spies*. New York: Doubleday, 1949.

FRANKLIN, CHARLES. *Spies of the Twentieth Century*. London: Odhams, 1967.

GOUZENKO, IGOR. *The Iron Curtain*. New York: Dutton, 1948.

GROVES, LESLIE R. *Now It Can Be Told*. New York: Harper, 1961.

HINCHLEY, VERNON. *Spies Who Never Were*. New York: Dodd Mead, 1965.

HUTTON, J. BERNARD. *School for Spies*. New York: Coward-McCann, 1962.

———— *The Traitor Trade*. New York: Obolensky, 1963.

KAZNACHEEV, ALEKSANDR. *Inside a Soviet Embassy*. Philadelphia: Lippincott, 1962.

KIRKPATRICK, LYMAN B., JR. *The Real CIA*. New York: Macmillan, 1967.

LOVELL, STANLEY P. *Of Spies and Stratagems*. New York: Prentice Hall, 1963.

MONTAGU, EWEN. *The Man Who Never Was*. Philadelphia: Lippincott, 1954.

MOOREHEAD, ALAN. *The Traitors*. New York: Scribner's, 1952.

OLLESTAD, NORMAN. *Inside the FBI*. New York: Lyle Stuart, 1967.

PENKOVSKIY, OLEG. *The Penkovskiy Papers*. New York: Doubleday, 1965.

PETROV, VLADIMIR, and EVDOKIA PETROVA. *Empire of Fear*. New York: Praeger, 1956.

PILAT, OLIVER. *The Atom Spies*. New York: Putnam, 1952.

PINTO, ORESTES. *Spy-Catcher*. New York: Harper, 1952.

ROOT, JONATHAN. *The Betrayers*. New York: Coward-McCann, 1962.

SANSOM, A. W. *I Spied Spies*. New York: International Publications, 1965.

SETH, RONALD. *Unmasked!: The Story of Soviet Espionage.* New York: Hawthorn, 1965.

——— *Spies at Work.* New York: Philosophical Library, 1955.

SHARP, MALCOM P. *Was Justice Done?* New York: Monthly Review Press, 1956.

TUCHMAN, BARBARA. *The Zimmermann Telegram.* New York: Macmillan, 1966.

TULLY, ANDREW. *CIA: The Inside Story.* New York: Morrow, 1962.

——— *The FBI's Most Famous Cases.* New York: Morrow, 1965.

WEST, REBECCA. *The Meaning of Treason.* New York: Viking, 1947.

WISE, DAVID, and THOMAS B. ROSS. *The Espionage Establishment.* New York: Random, 1967.

INDEX